COHERENCE UNIVERSALISM

COHERENCE UNIVERSALISM

Psychology

The Coherence Foundation of Psychological Life and the Meaning Crisis

Gaura Kiśora Dās Rader

Heaven≡Earth Press

Coherence Universalism Series • March 2026

Published by Heaven≡Earth Press
Athens, Ohio

Coherence Universalism Series

ISBN: 978-X-XXXX-XXXX-X (paperback)

This work is part of the Coherence Universalism framework. For the complete series and supporting materials, visit heavenearthfoundation.org.

Printed in the United States of America
First Edition: March 2026

Dedicated to the vision of a more coherent future
for all sentient beings

Acknowledgment

We acknowledge all those who have come before us. Your coherence is not lost, only lost to our vision. Our coherence is made possible only by your coherence.

Hexagram 13

Tóng Rén — Fellowship with People

Heaven above, Fire below

Fellowship with people in the open.
Success.
It furthers one to cross the great water.
Perseverance furthers.

Fire rises toward heaven: the image of fellowship among people. True community arises not from uniformity but from the clarity that comes when diverse people organize themselves around shared principles. The warmth of fire and the vastness of heaven together suggest that genuine fellowship must be open and inclusive — not confined to faction or clan, but extended to all who share in the common work.

Such fellowship succeeds because it rests on what people hold in common rather than what divides them. It has the strength to undertake great and difficult things — to cross the great water — precisely because its foundation is broad enough to sustain the weight. The perseverance required is not rigid adherence but steady commitment to the shared vision that brought people together in the first place.

— after the Yi Jing, Wilhelm/Baynes translation

Contents

Section 1: Introduction — Why Psychology Needs Coherence

Abstract

Abstract. This paper presents a unified psychological framework grounded in Coherence Universalism (CU), a philosophical and scientific framework that treats coherence — integrated order under constraint — as the organizing principle across physical, biological, psychological, social, and artificial systems. The central claim is that psychology is, at its foundation, the science of coherence: every canonical domain of the field — perception, cognition, memory, emotion, motivation, identity, attachment, personality, psychopathology, and therapy — can be understood as a mechanism that either supports or undermines the maintenance of integrated self-regulation across time. Coherence is not one concept among many that psychology employs. It is the structural constraint that determines whether psychological systems function, fragment, or collapse. The paper develops this claim across twelve substantive sections, introducing formal concepts specific to psychological coherence: meaning space and meaning maps (CU-Ψ1, CU-Ψ2), the Field Coherence Score (CU-Ψ3), Inverse Entropic Stress (CU-Ψ4), coherence drive (CU-Ψ5), local—global tension (CU-Ψ6), and the distinction between coherence collapse (pathology) and coherence divergence (neurodiversity). The framework reframes the contemporary mental health crisis as a systemic coherence crisis — a population-level condition in which coherence demands exceed available regulatory support — rather than an epidemic of individual pathology. It identifies self-deception (CU-Ψ11) as the structural precondition for moral failure and establishes the psychological foundations that CU — Ethics and CU — AI require. Eight appendices provide formal apparatus (meaning space, attractor dynamics), domain-specific analyses (gender, neurotransmitters, medications), the Coherence Ladder mapping, and a referenced principles index. All central claims are falsifiable, and the paper specifies the conditions under which the framework should be abandoned.

1.1 The State of the Field

Psychology is one of the most productive sciences of the past century and one of the least unified. Its subfields — cognitive science, clinical psychology, social psychology, developmental psychology, neuroscience, personality theory — have identified thousands of robust effects, constructed dozens of competing models, and generated interventions that alleviate real suffering. Yet the field remains without a shared foundational concept that explains why these phenomena belong together, why the interventions that work across schools share a common logic, or what holds a functioning mind together in the first place.

This is not a failure of effort or rigor. It is a consequence of the way psychology was constituted. Born in the late nineteenth century as an offshoot of philosophy and physiology, psychology inherited a division it has never resolved: between mechanistic explanation (how do cognitive processes work?) and experiential description (what is it like to be a person?). The field subsequently fragmented along methodological and institutional lines. Perception is studied separately from emotion. Cognition is modeled independently of identity. Therapy techniques are compared as competing schools rather than understood as variations on a common mechanism. Pathology is defined by deviation from statistical norms rather than by failure of integration.

The result is that psychology knows an extraordinary amount about the parts of the mind and remarkably little about what makes it whole.

1.2 The Preceding Framework

This paper is part of the Coherence Universalism (CU) series published by the Heaven≡Earth Press. It presupposes — and extends — the formal framework established in the preceding papers.

CU — M&E: The Transcendental Framework presents the Coherence Ladder, a sequence of structural rungs tracing the emergence of physical order, life, consciousness, meaning, social coordination, normativity, and governance from pure relational possibility. That paper establishes the foundational principles (CU-FP1 through CU-FP8) that govern coherence at every scale: that coherence is a transcendental condition (CU-FP1), that it admits of degree and direction (CU-FP2), that constraint is essential to its realization (CU-FP3), that it operates across multiple scales simultaneously (CU-FP4), and that identity is constraint-preserved coherence (CU-FP8).

CU — Consciousness develops the forcing conditions (CF-1 through CF-5) under which coherence acquires an interior — the conditions under which there is something it is like to be a system maintaining its own viability. That paper also establishes the identity conditions (CU-I1 through CU-I5), the seven structural conditions for consciousness (CU-C1 through CU-C7), the dynamics of coherence maintenance (CU-D1 through CU-D10), and the viability conditions (CU-V1 through CU-V7) that govern the felt dimension of experience. It introduces the **coherence functional** C(u) on state space H, the viability region V, the **distortion measure** D(u), and the Universal Flow Equation (CU-D1) that governs how conscious systems move through their **coherence landscape** s.

This psychological paper picks up where consciousness leaves off. The Consciousness paper asks: under what structural conditions does coherence become experience? This paper asks: once experience is in play, how do psychological systems maintain, lose, and restore coherence across time — and what happens when they cannot?

1.3 Position on the Coherence Ladder

The Coherence Ladder organizes the CU series by identifying which structural transitions each paper addresses. The Psychology paper occupies Rungs 16 through 26 — the span from internal models to culture — with particular focus on Rungs 19 through 24, where agency, meaning, and social coordination emerge.

— **Rungs 16–18** (Internal Models, Predictive Coherence, Error Correction) correspond to the perceptual, cognitive, and memorial processes treated in Section 2. These rungs establish the representational infrastructure that makes psychological coherence possible.

— **Rung 19** (Agency) corresponds to the self and identity structures treated in Section 4. Agency is the point at which coherence becomes something the system does rather than something that merely happens to it.

— **Rung 20** (Subjective Time) underlies the temporal extension of identity — the capacity to integrate past, present, and future into a single coherent trajectory, treated in Sections 5 and 10.

— **Rung 21** (Meaning) is the central psychological rung. Meaning arises when elements of experience are evaluated in terms of their relevance to coherence preservation across futures. It is the subject of Sections 4, 8, and Appendix B, where the formal concepts of meaning space and meaning maps are introduced.

— **Rungs 22–24** (Shared Representations, Coordination Dynamics, Norm Formation) correspond to the social and cultural dimensions of psychological coherence treated in Sections 9 and 9.

— **Rungs 25–26** (Institutions, Culture) extend the analysis to the collective structures that scaffold individual coherence, treated in Sections 10 and 10.

The physical rungs (1–10), biological rungs (11–15), and normative rungs (27–31) are presupposed or referenced but not developed here. They belong to other papers in the series.

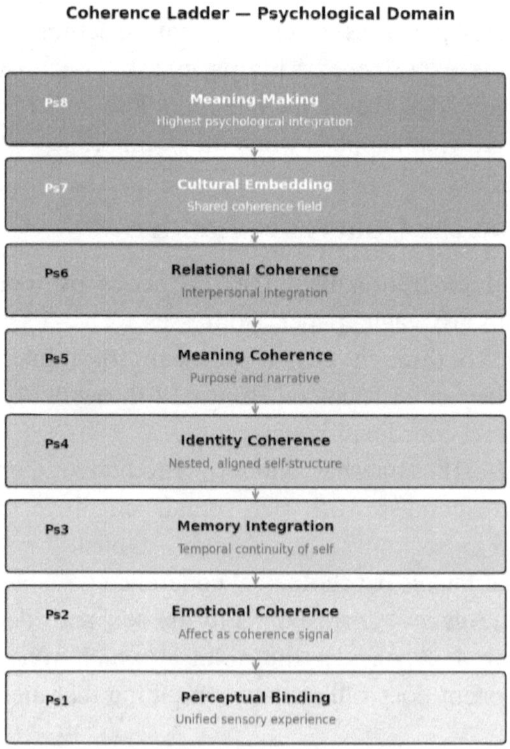

Coherence Ladder — Psychological Domain

Ps8 **Meaning-Making** — Highest psychological integration
Ps7 **Cultural Embedding** — Shared coherence field
Ps6 **Relational Coherence** — Interpersonal integration
Ps5 **Meaning Coherence** — Purpose and narrative
Ps4 **Identity Coherence** — Nested, aligned self-structure
Ps3 **Memory Integration** — Temporal continuity of self
Ps2 **Emotional Coherence** — Affect as coherence signal
Ps1 **Perceptual Binding** — Unified sensory experience

Figure 1. *The Coherence Ladder in psychological context. Psychology occupies the upper rungs of the ladder, from perceptual binding (CU-C2, perspectival unity)* *through meaning coherence. Each rung enables and constrains those above it: emotional coherence requires perceptual coherence, identity coherence requires emotional coherence, and so on. The framework treats these as structural levels of integration rather than independent domains.*

1.4 The Central Claim

This paper advances a simple but far-reaching thesis: **psychology is, at its foundation, the science of coherence**.

Every canonical domain of psychology — perception, cognition, memory, emotion, motivation, identity, attachment, personality, psychopathology, therapy — can be understood as a mechanism that either supports or undermines the maintenance of integrated self-regulation across time. Coherence is not one concept among many that psychology employs. It is the structural constraint that determines whether psychological systems function, fragment, or collapse.

This claim is not a metaphor. It connects directly to the formal apparatus of Coherence Universalism:

— The coherence functional C(u) introduced in the Consciousness paper continues to apply. Psychological states are configurations in a state space, and their coherence is measurable in principle.

— The dynamics principles CU-D2 and CU-D3 (coherence drive) manifest psychologically as the system's felt sensitivity to misalignment and its impulse to restore integration — experienced as tension, curiosity, anxiety, motivation, or longing.

— The gradient navigation principle CU-D4 explains why psychological systems routinely sacrifice global coherence for local relief — why the short-term choice that reduces anxiety may increase long-term fragmentation.

— The multi-scale coherence principle CU-FP4 explains why conflicts between local and global coherence are the structural signature of nearly every form of psychological suffering.

— The identity conditions CU-I1 through CU-I5 ground the analysis of personality, self-models, and the conditions under which identity coherence is preserved or lost.

This paper extends the formal framework by introducing concepts specific to psychological coherence: meaning space, meaning maps, the Field Coherence Score (FCS), Inverse Entropic Stress (IES), and attractor dominance profiles. These are assigned principle numbers CU-Ψ1 through CU-Ψ12 and developed in the appendices.

1.5 The Mental Health Crisis as a Coherence Crisis

This paper is not motivated by theoretical curiosity alone. It responds to an emergency.

By every available measure, the psychological condition of modern populations is deteriorating. Depression, anxiety, substance use disorders, loneliness, and suicidality have risen dramatically across developed nations over the past two decades, with acceleration since 2010 and sharp intensification since 2020. Among adolescents, the crisis is acute: rates of self-harm and suicidal ideation have doubled or tripled in many countries within a generation. These trends are not confined to any single demographic, culture, or economic stratum.

Current responses — expanded access to therapy, pharmacological intervention, public awareness campaigns, digital mental health tools — are valuable but insufficient. They treat psychological distress as an individual condition requiring individual repair, while the evidence increasingly suggests that the crisis is systemic. Individuals are not breaking down because they are individually defective. They are breaking down because the coherence demands placed on them exceed the coherence support available to them.

Coherence Universalism explains why.

The modern environment is characterized by unprecedented informational density, continuous social comparison, rapid disruption of inherited meaning structures, erosion of institutional trust, and algorithmic systems optimized for engagement rather than integration. Each of these forces elevates Inverse Entropic Stress (IES) — the pressure placed on a psychological system when coherence demands exceed regulatory capacity. Simultaneously, the structures that historically scaffolded individual coherence — stable communities, shared narratives, intergenerational relationships, religious and civic institutions — have weakened or fragmented, reducing the distributed coherence support (Rungs 22–26) that humans evolved to depend on.

The result is a population-level coherence crisis in which:

— Individual systems are asked to maintain coherence across more domains, faster changes, and more contradictory demands than at any point in human history.

— The social and cultural structures that normally distribute **regulatory load** across groups (Rung 22–26) have degraded, forcing individuals to carry loads that were never designed to be borne alone.

— Technologies optimized for local engagement (dopamine-gradient exploitation) systematically degrade global coherence, creating the paradox of a population that is more stimulated and less integrated than ever before.

— Therapeutic interventions, however effective at the individual level, cannot compensate for collapsing collective coherence. A therapist can restore one meaning map; a therapist cannot rebuild the shared coherence field.

This analysis is not pessimistic. It is diagnostic — and it points toward solutions that are currently invisible within the standard clinical framework.

If the mental health crisis is fundamentally a coherence crisis, then sustainable solutions must operate at the level of coherence, not merely at the level of symptoms. This means:

— **Clinical practice** must be reframed around coherence restoration rather than symptom reduction. The question shifts from "What disorder does this person have?" to "Where and how has coherence failed, and what would support reintegration?"

— **Institutional design** must be evaluated by its effects on the coherence of the populations it serves. Education, employment, housing, media, and governance are all coherence-modulating systems, and their design has psychological consequences that current frameworks largely ignore.

— **Technology design** must be constrained by coherence preservation. Systems that systematically degrade human coherence — even while improving efficiency, convenience, or engagement — impose costs that show up as psychological distress, and those costs are currently externalized onto individuals and healthcare systems.

— **Research priorities** must shift toward understanding coherence at the system level, not only at the individual level. Population-level coherence metrics (aggregate FCS, distributed IES, shared coherence field stability) would allow the field to track what matters rather than counting diagnoses.

The subsequent sections of this paper provide the theoretical foundation for this reorientation. They do not attempt to teach psychology or exhaustively review its subfields. Instead, they show that coherence appears wherever psychology is doing its best explanatory work — and that coherence collapse appears wherever psychology confronts its most difficult problems.

1.6 What This Paper Does and Does Not Claim

This paper claims that coherence is the best foundational concept for psychology — the structural constraint that unifies perception, cognition, emotion, identity, psychopathology, and therapy into a single explanatory framework. It claims that making this concept explicit resolves longstanding fragmentation in the field and reframes the contemporary mental health crisis as a systemic coherence crisis rather than an epidemic of individual pathology.

This paper does not claim that coherence replaces existing psychological constructs. Reinforcement, attachment, cognitive schemas, neural circuits, and personality traits remain real and important. The claim is that these constructs become more intelligible — and their interactions more predictable — when understood as aspects of a single coherence dynamics rather than as competing partial theories.

The mathematical formalisms introduced here — meaning space, the Field Coherence Score, Inverse Entropic Stress, attractor dominance profiles — are offered as structural proposals, not as finished quantitative models. They have been developed in good faith and checked for formal plausibility, but they await the empirical operationalization and quantitative testing that would establish them as measurement instruments. The framework is precise enough to be wrong — and Section 0.8 specifies what observations would falsify its central claims.

Finally, this paper does not attempt to replace clinical judgment with formal calculation. Coherence dynamics provides a unifying logic for understanding why interventions work, when they fail, and what genuine recovery consists in. It does not prescribe treatment protocols or override the relational and contextual sensitivity that effective clinical work requires.

1.7 Structure of the Paper

The paper proceeds by organizing the canonical domains of psychology around the function they serve in maintaining coherence, rather than around historical subdisciplines.

Sections 2–2 establish what coherence means in a psychological system and examine perception, cognition, and memory as mechanisms of pattern integration.

Sections 4–4 treat emotion and motivation as regulatory signaling systems, and identity and personality as long-horizon coherence structures.

Section 6 examines sexuality, attachment, and intimacy as mechanisms of interpersonal coherence.

Section 7 addresses trauma, neurodiversity, and psychopathology through the coherence collapse / coherence divergence distinction.

Section 8 reframes therapy, healing practices, and psychoactive substances as coherence modulation.

Sections 9–9 extend the analysis to moral, political, and meaning systems, and to group psychology, culture, and religion as shared coherence fields.

Section 11 situates psychological coherence within developmental, evolutionary, and historical time.

Section 12 makes the explanatory case explicit: why coherence is the best foundational concept for psychology.

Section 13 articulates transitions to the Ethics and AI papers.

The appendices provide formal development (meaning space, FCS, IES, attractor dynamics), domain-specific analyses (gender, neurotransmitters, medications), empirical testability, the Coherence Ladder position mapping, and a glossary.

The central claim of this paper is simple but consequential: psychology has always been the study of how minds maintain coherence over time. Making this explicit does not narrow the field. It finally unifies it — and in doing so, reveals both why the current crisis runs so deep and what genuine progress would require.

1.8 What Would Prove This Framework Wrong

Coherence Universalism's psychological claims are offered as falsifiable proposals. The framework would be substantially undermined if any of the following were demonstrated:

Therapeutic equivalence without coherence mechanism. If a class of effective psychological interventions could be identified whose mechanism of action does not involve coherence restoration — that is, interventions that reliably improve psychological functioning without increasing integration across meaning-map domains, reducing distortion D(u), or restoring gradient navigability — this would refute the claim that coherence is the common mechanism underlying therapeutic change (Section 8).

Pathology without coherence failure. If persistent psychological suffering were shown to occur in systems that maintain high global coherence — systems with integrated meaning maps, navigable gradients, and low IES — this would refute the claim that psychopathology is fundamentally coherence failure (Section 7). The framework predicts that suffering without coherence degradation does not occur at clinically significant timescales.

Incoherence without functional cost. If sustained meaning-map fragmentation, elevated IES, or chronic local—global tension could be shown to be psychologically neutral — producing no measurable effects on agency, identity stability, or well-being — this would refute the claim that coherence is functionally necessary for psychological health.

Developmental trajectories that bypass integration. If mature psychological functioning — flexible agency, stable identity, moral reasoning, relational capacity — could be shown to develop without the progressive integration of coherence attractors described in Appendix F, this would undermine the developmental model and its implications for understanding both normal maturation and arrested development.

Section 12 develops the explanatory case in full. Appendix B provides the formal apparatus against which these conditions can be operationalized.

Section 2: What Coherence Means in a Psychological System

The Consciousness paper established that coherence, under certain structural conditions, is not merely correlated with experience but constitutive of it. The forcing conditions (CF-1 through CF-5) specify when coherence acquires an interior; the structural conditions (CU-C1 through CU-C7) specify what that interior consists in; the dynamics principles (CU-D1 through CU-D10) specify how conscious systems move through their coherence landscapes.

This paper takes up a different but equally fundamental question: once a system is conscious — once coherence has become experience — how does it maintain, lose, and restore that coherence across the timescales and domains that constitute a psychological life?

The answer requires translating the formal apparatus of coherence into the specific vocabulary of psychological functioning. This section establishes the key concepts.

2.1 Psychological Coherence as System-Level Integration

A psychological system is not a single mechanism. It is an ensemble of coupled processes — perception, emotion, cognition, memory, motivation, embodiment, and social attunement — that must operate together across time. Coherence, in the psychological sense, refers to the degree to which these processes mutually support one another rather than interfere or fragment.

This is a direct extension of the foundational principle CU-FP1 (Coherence as Transcendental Condition) into the psychological domain. Just as coherence is the condition of possibility for anything to count as a structured entity at all, psychological coherence is the condition of possibility for anything to count as a functioning mind. A collection of cognitive processes that cannot integrate — that perceives without remembering, emotes without regulating, or acts without self-monitoring — does not constitute a mind in any psychologically meaningful sense. It constitutes a set of disconnected operations.

In a coherent psychological system: perception aligns with action; emotion provides usable regulatory information; cognition integrates rather than overrides affect; memory supports continuity rather than intrusion; identity stabilizes choice across time; and behavior remains intelligible to the agent herself. Coherence is therefore not a property of any one subsystem. It is, as the consciousness conditions already specify (CU-C1, Global Integrative Coherence), a system-level achievement.

The formal apparatus introduced in the Consciousness paper carries over directly. A psychological system occupies a configuration u in a state space H. The coherence functional C(u) measures the degree of integrated mutual constraint across the system's components at that configuration. (Here u denotes a psychological state; C(u) is the domain-specific notation for the general coherence functional C(x) introduced in the Physics and Biology papers, specialized to the psychological state space.) The viability region $V \subset H$ defines the set of configurations in which the system's identity conditions (CU-I1 through CU-I5) remain satisfied — the region the system must not leave if it is to persist as this system. Psychological functioning occurs within V; psychological crisis occurs near its boundaries; psychological collapse occurs when the boundary is crossed.

What the Psychology paper adds is the recognition that for systems of human complexity, V is not a simple region but a high-dimensional landscape with multiple local optima, saddle points, and basins of attraction. The system does not merely need to stay within V; it must navigate V across rapidly shifting conditions — social demands, bodily states, informational load, relational rupture, developmental transition — without falling into configurations that are locally stable but globally degraded. This navigational challenge is the subject matter of psychology. Crucially, it cannot be reduced to the biological or conscious-level processes from which it emerges — the foundational principle CU-FP5 (Non-Reductive Emergence) holds here with full force. Psychological coherence depends on neural, bodily, and phenomenal substrates but is not predictable from or reducible to any of them.

2.2 Local and Global Coherence (CU-Ψ6)

The most consequential structural feature of psychological coherence is that it operates across multiple scales simultaneously. This follows directly from CU-FP4 (Multi-Scale Coherence), but in the psychological domain it takes a specific and clinically central form.

CU-Ψ6. Local—Global Coherence Tension. Psychological systems maintain coherence at multiple scales — within individual domains (perceptual, emotional, cognitive, relational) and across domains over time. Local coherence refers to short-term alignment within a limited domain. Global coherence refers to integration across domains, timescales, and identity commitments. These scales can and routinely do conflict, and the structural tension between them is the primary source of psychological suffering.

Local coherence is real and often necessary. A belief may feel internally consistent. An emotion may motivate decisive action. A coping strategy may reduce immediate distress. A relationship may stabilize identity. Each of these represents genuine coherence — integration that the system has achieved within a particular domain or timescale.

Global coherence is integration that spans domains and persists across time. A globally coherent system maintains alignment not only within a moment but between past commitments, present actions, future consequences, embodied needs, and social realities.

The tension between local and global coherence is the engine of most psychological difficulty. An action that reduces anxiety now may undermine identity later. A belief that stabilizes meaning may distort perception. A strategy that preserves attachment may sacrifice agency. A substance that restores calm may erode regulatory capacity. In each case, the system achieves coherence at one scale by sacrificing it at another.

This is not a flaw in the system. It is a consequence of CU-D4 (Gradient Navigation Under Constraint). Psychological systems do not optimize globally — they follow local gradients, responding to nearby slopes in the coherence landscape. A system may climb a local gradient while descending a global one. The Consciousness paper identified this as the structural basis of conscious fallibility; in psychology, it is the structural basis of self-defeating behavior, addiction, rationalization, and the persistence of suffering despite intelligence and good intention.

Festinger's (1957) cognitive dissonance theory captures one face of this tension: the discomfort produced by simultaneously holding contradictory beliefs, and the motivated distortion that follows. But dissonance is only one instance of the general principle. The tension between local and global coherence manifests across every psychological domain — not only in belief, but in emotion, identity, attachment, and meaning. CU-Ψ6 identifies the structural constraint that dissonance, ambivalence, self-deception, and motivational conflict all instantiate.

2.3 Coherence Drive in Psychological Systems (CU-Ψ5)

Psychological systems do not merely possess coherence. They actively seek it. The Consciousness paper formalized this as coherence drive (CU-D2, CU-D3): the descriptive tendency of persisting systems to maintain or recover coherence. In biological systems, this appears as active regulation, repair, and reorganization in response to disruption. In experience, it appears as the restlessness of unresolved tension, the relief of integration, and the aversiveness of fragmentation.

In the psychological domain, coherence drive takes a specific and pervasive form:

CU-Ψ5. Psychological Coherence Drive. Conscious psychological systems exhibit a felt sensitivity to misalignment across their component processes and a persistent impulse to restore integration. This drive is experienced as tension, discomfort, curiosity, anxiety, motivation, or longing, depending on the domain and timescale of the threatened coherence.

CU-Ψ5 is the psychological instantiation of CU-D2/D3, not a separate principle. What it adds is specificity about how coherence drive manifests in systems complex enough to maintain meaning, identity, and social bonds across extended time.

This reframes many familiar psychological phenomena. Anxiety is not free-floating distress but sensitivity to impending or actual incoherence — the felt registration that something in the system's integration is failing or about to fail. Motivation is not a separate force that drives behavior from outside the cognitive system but movement along **coherence gradient** s — the system's response to perceived opportunities for integration or restoration. Meaning-seeking is not an optional luxury layered onto basic drives but long-horizon coherence repair — the attempt to restore integration across values, identity, and future orientation when shorter-horizon strategies have proved insufficient. Boredom signals that the system's current configuration offers no coherence gradient to follow — no direction in which things could get better or more integrated. Depression often reflects a state in which coherence drive remains active (the system still registers that things are wrong) but perceived pathways for restoration are blocked, producing paralysis rather than action.

These are not metaphorical redescriptions. They follow from the formal structure: if psychological states are configurations in H, and if the system navigates by following ∇C (the coherence gradient), then the felt quality of experience at any moment reflects the local gradient structure — its steepness, its direction, and whether viable paths exist.

2.4 Coherence Is Dynamic, Not Static

Coherence is not something a psychological system achieves once and then possesses. It must be continuously maintained against perturbation. This follows from the Universal Flow Equation (CU-D1): the system's configuration is always evolving, always being updated in response to internal dynamics and external input. New information, social pressures, bodily states, developmental transitions, and environmental changes constantly threaten integration.

This dynamic quality explains why psychological stability is fragile — and why its fragility is not a defect but a structural necessity. A system that could not be perturbed would be rigid, not coherent. Genuine coherence requires what CU-D7 (Novelty Through Constraint Navigation) describes: the capacity to discover new configurations in response to new challenges, finding solutions that are constrained but not predetermined. Psychological resilience is not resistance to perturbation but the capacity to reorganize coherently after perturbation — to find new viable configurations within V rather than fragmenting or rigidifying.

This is why high coherence does not imply rigidity. In fact, rigid systems often maintain the appearance of coherence at the cost of adaptability. A person whose beliefs never change, whose identity admits no revision, and whose behavior follows fixed scripts may appear stable. But rigidity is a coherence strategy with a characteristic failure mode: when conditions shift beyond the system's narrow tolerance, there is no capacity for reorganization. The result is brittle collapse rather than graceful adaptation. Piaget's (1954) accommodation — the revision of cognitive structures in response to experience that cannot be assimilated — is the developmental expression of this principle. Systems that only assimilate without accommodating achieve local coherence at the cost of progressive disconnection from reality.

The dynamic character of coherence also explains why psychological change is often nonlinear. Therapeutic growth, developmental transition, and recovery from trauma frequently involve temporary destabilization — increased anxiety, confusion, or loss of familiar identity structures — before reintegration at a higher level. This is not a side effect of change; it is the structural signature of transition between coherence configurations. The system must leave one basin of attraction in V before it can settle into another, and the transit between basins is inherently destabilizing.

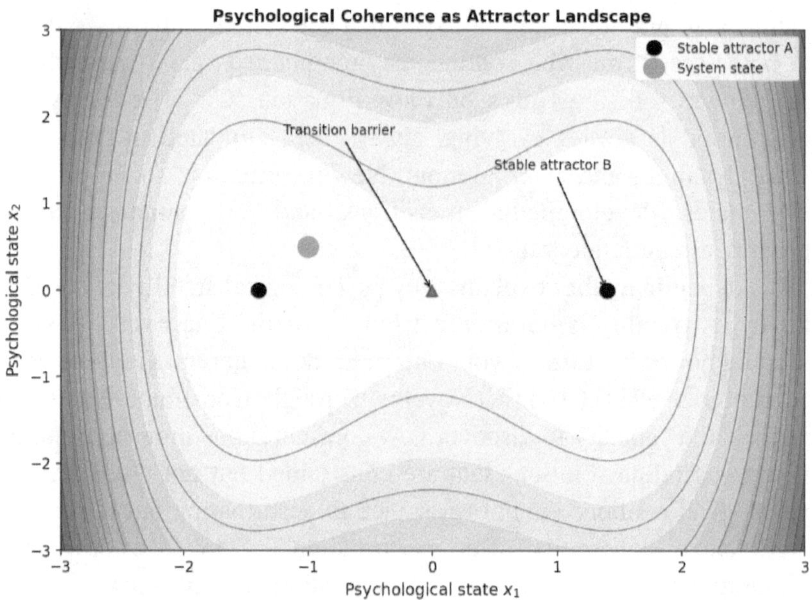

Figure 2. Psychological coherence as an attractor landscape. Stable psychological configurations correspond to minima in the coherence landscape. The transition barrier between attractors represents the energetic cost of reorganization. A system (grey ball) may be displaced from its attractor by perturbation but returns unless the perturbation exceeds the barrier height. Therapy, trauma, and developmental transitions can all be modeled as movements across this landscape.

2.5 Coherence as a Constraint, Not an Ideal

Finally, coherence should not be understood as an idealized state of harmony or perfection. It is a constraint on viable functioning — a specification of what any psychological system must respect in order to remain agentive, intelligible, and capable of sustained action over time.

This distinction is critical. Coherence does not prescribe what a person should value, believe, or become. It does not privilege any particular personality type, cultural tradition, or way of life. It specifies the structural conditions that any viable psychological organization must satisfy, just as the viability conditions (CU-V1 through CU-V7) specify what any conscious system must maintain to remain conscious.

The analogy to physical viability is instructive. Biological organisms can take an enormous variety of forms — from bacteria to blue whales — but all must maintain metabolic coherence, membrane integrity, and energy throughput. The constraint does not determine the form; it determines what forms are possible. Similarly, psychological systems can pursue radically different goals, organize around different values, and express different identities, but they cannot violate coherence indefinitely without cost. Systems that systematically distort perception, suppress regulatory signals, fragment memory, or sacrifice long-horizon integration for short-term relief pay a price that shows up as suffering, dysfunction, and eventual collapse.

This is why coherence functions as a foundational explanatory concept rather than a normative doctrine. It explains why certain patterns of psychological organization are sustainable and others are not, without dictating what the sustainable patterns must contain. It provides a criterion — viability of integrated functioning — that applies across cultures, personalities, and value systems without reducing to any of them.

This section has defined psychological coherence as the sustained integration of regulatory processes across seven meaning-space dimensions — emotional, narrative, relational, motivational, value, identity, and existential. The coherence functional C(x), the Field Coherence Score, and Inverse Entropic Stress (CU-Ψ3, CU-Ψ4) provide measurable quantities that track psychological integration and its breakdown. This framework treats coherence as explanatory rather than normative: it explains why certain patterns of organization are sustainable and others are not.

Section 3: Perception, Cognition, and Memory — Coherence as Pattern Integration

Perception, cognition, and memory are conventionally treated as distinct faculties, studied by separate subfields and modeled using different mechanisms. From the perspective of Coherence Universalism, they are better understood as tightly coupled components of a single function: the integration of patterns across time and context in service of psychological coherence.

This function corresponds to Rungs 16 through 18 on the Coherence Ladder. Rung 16 (Internal Models) establishes that living systems maintain compressed representations of themselves and their environments — representations that allow them to distinguish internal from external states and anticipate how changes will affect coherence. Rung 17 (Predictive Coherence) establishes that coherence is evaluated relative to anticipated future states, not only present stability. Rung 18 (Error Correction) establishes that discrepancies between predicted and actual outcomes drive updates to internal models, making learning structurally unavoidable.

Perception, cognition, and memory are the psychological processes through which these structural capacities are realized in human systems. They are not information-processing modules operating in isolation. They are coherence-preserving mechanisms that allow psychological systems to make sense of the world without disintegrating under its complexity.

3.1 Perception as Coherence Construction

Perception is not a passive recording of sensory input. It is an active process of organizing signals into stable, meaningful patterns — an ongoing construction of coherence from inherently noisy and incomplete data.

This is now well established empirically. The predictive processing framework (Clark, 2013; Friston, 2010; Hohwy, 2013) characterizes perception as a process of hierarchical prediction: the brain generates top-down predictions about incoming sensory signals and processes primarily the discrepancies — prediction errors — between expectation and input. What reaches conscious awareness is not raw data but a best-guess model that integrates prior expectation with current evidence to produce a coherent perceptual field.

CU grounds this empirical picture in a deeper structural necessity. Perceptual systems prioritize coherence because coherence is not an optional feature of perception but the condition of its possibility (CU-FP1). Sensory information, unintegrated, is not merely impoverished — it is unusable. A visual field that cannot resolve figure from ground, an auditory stream that cannot distinguish signal from noise, a proprioceptive system that cannot distinguish self-generated from externally caused movement: these are not degraded perception but the absence of perception. Perception occurs only when signals are integrated into a coherent representation that the system can act upon.

This is why perception is context-sensitive, predictive, and vulnerable to illusion. These features are not bugs in the perceptual system — they are consequences of the system's commitment to coherence. Illusions arise precisely where the system's coherence-preserving strategies produce interpretations that diverge from physical reality. The Müller-Lyer illusion, the Kanizsa triangle, binocular rivalry — these demonstrate that perception will fabricate coherence where the stimulus does not fully support it, because an incoherent percept is functionally worse than an inaccurate one.

The connection to the Consciousness paper is direct. The Consciousness paper's engagement with predictive processing (Section 3.3) argued that CU is highly compatible with PP: both emphasize regulation over representation; both see the brain as a coherence-maintaining system. What CU adds is the forcing conditions that specify when prediction error becomes felt valence — when it matters to the system, not merely in a functional sense but in an experiential one (CF-2, Identity-Relevant Stakes). In the psychological domain, this means that perceptual coherence is not merely computationally achieved; it is experienced. The coherence of a visual scene feels stable. Perceptual breakdown feels disorienting. The system does not merely model coherence — it lives it.

3.2 Cognition as Higher-Order Coherence Maintenance

Where perception integrates patterns across space and modality, cognition integrates patterns across representations. Reasoning, problem-solving, categorization, and abstraction are coherence-maintenance strategies operating at a higher level of organization. They allow the system to reconcile competing interpretations, resolve contradictions, and construct models that remain stable across changing circumstances.

This view of cognition follows from the Ladder's structural logic. Rung 16 (Internal Models) establishes the basic capacity for compressed representation. Rung 17 (Predictive Coherence) adds temporal projection — the ability to evaluate present configurations relative to anticipated futures. Cognition, in this framework, is the suite of operations that maintain and extend the coherence of internal models across representational complexity: across levels of abstraction, across domains of knowledge, across the competing demands of accuracy and utility.

From this perspective, many phenomena that psychology classifies as cognitive failure become intelligible as coherence strategy. Confirmation bias — the tendency to seek and favor evidence that supports existing beliefs — is a local coherence strategy (CU-Ψ6): it preserves the coherence of the current belief structure by filtering inputs that would destabilize it. Anchoring effects reflect the system's tendency to maintain coherence with initial reference points rather than recomputing from scratch. The availability heuristic reflects the system's use of easily integrated (i.e., coherent) examples over statistically representative ones.

Kahneman and Tversky's (1974) research program on heuristics and biases documented these patterns extensively but framed them as departures from rational norms. CU offers a different interpretation: they are not departures from rationality but expressions of a system that prioritizes coherence over accuracy when the two conflict. The system is not failing to be rational; it is succeeding at being coherent — locally. The pathology arises not from the heuristic itself but from the gap between local and global coherence (CU-Ψ6), which Kahneman (2011) later approximated with his System 1 / System 2 framework. What Kahneman describes as the substitution of easy questions for hard ones is, in CU terms, the system's preference for configurations that can be integrated quickly (local coherence) over configurations that would require costly reorganization (global coherence).

This reframing has a significant implication: irrationality is not the fundamental category. Coherence failure is. A person who holds contradictory beliefs is not failing at logic; she is managing a coherence landscape in which the contradictions cannot be resolved without destabilizing identity, relationships, or meaning. The contradiction persists because resolving it would cost more coherence than maintaining it. This is precisely the local-versus-global tradeoff described by CU-D4 (Gradient Navigation Under Constraint): the system ascends the local gradient (belief stability) while descending the global one (epistemic integrity).

3.3 Memory as Temporal Coherence

Memory extends coherence across time. Psychological systems are temporally extended — they must integrate past experiences, present states, and future expectations into a single navigable structure. Without memory, there can be no sustained identity, no learning, no agency, and no meaning. Memory is therefore not a storage system; it is the mechanism of temporal coherence (CU-C5).

This corresponds directly to the Coherence Ladder's account of Rung 18 (Error Correction) and Rung 20 (Subjective Time). Error correction requires that the system retain traces of past predictions and their outcomes in order to update its models. Subjective time requires that memory, prediction, and present experience be integrated into a unified internal narrative. Memory serves both functions: it provides the substrate for model updating and the material for temporal self-construction.

The reconstructive nature of memory — well established since Bartlett (1932) and extensively documented in modern research (Schacter, 1996; Loftus, 2005) — is often framed as a deficiency. Memories are not veridical recordings but active reconstructions, shaped by present context, emotion, and self-concept. From a pure information-storage perspective, this looks like a flaw. From a coherence perspective, it is a functional necessity.

Perfect fidelity would overwhelm integration. A system that recalled every detail of every experience with equal vividness and accessibility would be unable to construct the selective, structured narrative that identity requires. The reconstructive character of memory is the temporal analogue of perceptual construction: just as perception fabricates coherence from noisy sensory data, memory fabricates coherence from noisy temporal data. Both sacrifice accuracy for integrability.

This is why memory is so deeply entangled with identity. The narrative self (McAdams, 2001; Bruner, 1990) is not a fiction imposed on memory but the coherence structure that memory serves. Memories are retained, modified, and organized in ways that support the current self-model. This is functional when the self-model is flexible enough to accommodate new experience. It becomes pathological when the self-model is so rigid that memory must be continuously distorted to preserve it — the mechanism of self-deception described in Section 2.2 and formalized in Appendix B.

3.3.1 Memory as Constraint Deformation

The reconstructive account captures memory's phenomenology — how remembering feels and what it produces. But CU offers a deeper structural characterization: memory is not primarily a record of what happened; it is a deformation of the system's viable future trajectories.

Every significant experience reshapes the landscape of actions, interpretations, and responses that the system treats as admissible. A child who learns that fire burns does not merely store a fact; the child's space of viable behaviors has been permanently narrowed — reaching into flames is no longer a live option. A person who discovers betrayal in an intimate relationship does not merely acquire a painful memory; the range of futures the person treats as safe has been restructured. The memory is not the stored content but the reshaped constraint.

This distinction — between informational memory and constraint memory — has precise implications. Informational memory asks: *what happened?* It stores events, facts, and narratives that can be retrieved and reported. Constraint memory asks: *what kinds of actions still make sense?* It encodes the accumulated deformation of the system's navigational structure — the goals that survived conflict, the strategies that stabilized, the boundaries discovered through failure, the interpretive patterns shaped by repeated experience. A person does not replay her entire life history before making a decision. She operates from within a shaped behavioral manifold — a constraint structure that is the accumulated residue of everything she has lived through.

This reframing explains several features of memory that informational models struggle with. It explains why procedural and implicit memory often outlast explicit recall — because constraint deformation persists even when the specific events that produced it are no longer accessible to consciousness. It explains why amnesia patients can retain personality, preference, and skill while losing autobiographical narrative — because the constraint structure can survive damage to the informational layer. And it explains what is actually preserved when memory is "reconstructed": not the original event but the navigational structure it produced. The reconstruction serves present coherence because that is what memory is *for* — not fidelity to the past but viability in the future.

The constraint-memory concept also clarifies the relationship between memory and identity developed formally in Section 4. If memory is constraint deformation and identity is the persistence of constraint structure across time, then memory and identity are not separate phenomena that happen to interact; they are two descriptions of the same underlying process. Memory is how the constraint structure was shaped; identity is the structure as it persists. A system that loses its constraint memory — through neurodegeneration, catastrophic dissociation, or radical disruption — does not merely forget its past; it loses the navigational structure that made it *this* particular agent. This connection will prove critical for understanding trauma (Section 7), where the traumatic event does not merely deposit a painful memory but forces a discontinuous restructuring of the constraint manifold itself.

3.4 Failures of Temporal Coherence

Failures of memory-based coherence produce characteristic pathologies, each of which can be precisely located within the formal framework.

Intrusive memories — the hallmark of post-traumatic stress — reflect failures of temporal integration. The traumatic experience has not been incorporated into the system's narrative structure; it remains unintegrated, erupting into present awareness as if it were still occurring. In formal terms, the memory trace occupies a region of state space H that cannot be connected to the system's current coherence configuration without crossing the viability boundary of V. The system cannot integrate the memory because integration would destabilize identity (CU-I5, Identity Collapse Thresholds). The memory therefore persists as an encapsulated fragment — locally coherent (it retains its own internal organization) but globally disruptive (it cannot be incorporated into the temporal structure that supports the self).

Rumination — the repetitive, involuntary rehearsal of negative events or concerns — reflects a different failure: the system's coherence drive (CU-Ψ5) is engaged but cannot find a viable gradient. The system detects incoherence (something unresolved, something threatening) and attempts to repair it through cognitive reprocessing, but the reprocessing never reaches resolution because the underlying coherence conflict is not cognitive — it is emotional, relational, or identity-level. Rumination is coherence drive without a navigable path.

Confabulation — the construction of false memories to fill gaps — reflects the system's intolerance of temporal incoherence. When memory fails, the system generates plausible reconstructions that preserve narrative continuity (CU-C5, temporal thickness). This is not lying or delusion; it is the temporal analogue of perceptual gap-filling, driven by the same structural commitment to coherence that makes normal perception possible.

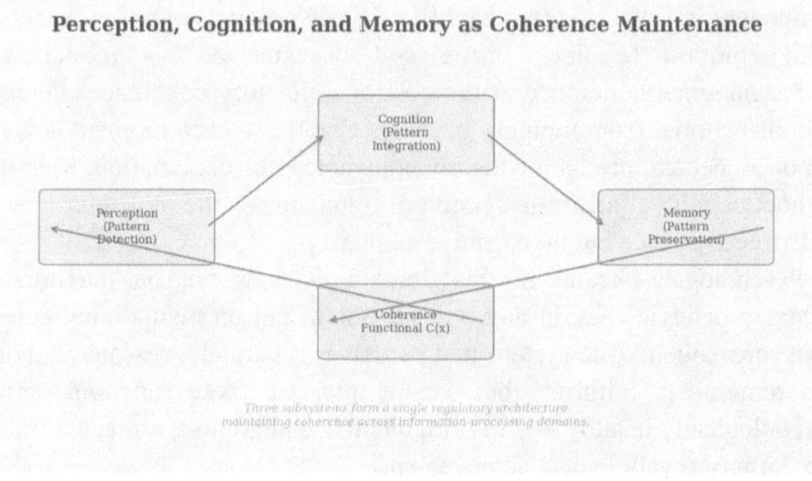

Figure 3. *The perception–cognition–memory integration cycle. Perception constructs local coherence from sensory input; cognition maintains higher-order coherence across domains; memory provides temporal coherence. All three operate as coupled subsystems with bidirectional constraint flow.*

3.5 The Integration Requirement

Perception, cognition, and memory do not operate independently. Perceptual expectations shape what is noticed. Cognitive models shape how experiences are interpreted. Memory shapes both perception and cognition by providing the narrative continuity within which new experience is embedded. Coherence emerges only when these processes mutually constrain one another — when each process is informed by and responsive to the others.

This mutual constraint is what the Consciousness paper describes as global integrative coherence (CU-C1): the requirement that information be integrated across the system rather than processed in isolated modules. In the psychological domain, CU-C1 manifests as the requirement that perception, cognition, and memory converge on a single coherent interpretation of the world and the agent's place in it. When they converge, experience is stable and action is possible. When they diverge — when perception reports one thing, memory another, and cognition a third — the system enters a state of elevated distortion D(u) that must be resolved or contained.

This integrated view explains why attempts to optimize one component in isolation often backfire. Hyper-rational cognition detached from emotion becomes brittle and disconnected — it achieves representational coherence at the cost of regulatory coherence. Perception unanchored from memory becomes chaotic — each moment is vivid but unconnected, producing the phenomenology of dissociation. Memory without cognitive integration becomes traumatic — the past returns with full affective force but no narrative context.

Psychological health in this domain depends not on maximizing accuracy or efficiency in any one subsystem but on maintaining coherence across them. The system that perceives accurately, reasons soundly, and remembers faithfully but cannot integrate these functions is not psychologically healthy — it is fragmented. Integration, not accuracy, is the primary psychological achievement.

This section has shown that perception, cognition, and memory operate as coherence maintenance systems — not isolated information-processing modules but integrated components of a single regulatory architecture. Psychological health in this domain depends not on maximizing accuracy or efficiency in any one subsystem but on maintaining coherence across them.

Section 4: Emotion and Motivation — Coherence as Regulatory Signaling

Emotion and motivation are treated ambivalently within psychology. They are recognized as central to behavior, decision-making, and well-being, yet frequently framed as sources of bias, noise, or irrationality — forces that interfere with "pure" cognition. Behavioral economics models emotion as a departure from rational utility maximization. Cognitive psychology often treats affect as a confound to be controlled. Even clinical practice sometimes implies that emotional responses are problems to be managed rather than signals to be understood.

From the perspective of Coherence Universalism, this ambivalence reflects a category mistake. Emotion and motivation are not obstacles to coherence. They are the primary regulatory mechanisms through which psychological systems detect, evaluate, and respond to changes in coherence. They are, in the precise sense developed in the Consciousness paper, the felt dimension of coherence dynamics — the interior aspect of a system navigating its own viability landscape.

4.1 Valence as the Foundation of Emotion

The Consciousness paper established that valence — the felt quality of experience as positive or negative, good or bad, approach-worthy or aversion-worthy — is not an epiphenomenal gloss added to neutral cognitive processing. It is the interior aspect of the system's movement along coherence gradients (CU-C3, Valence as Ineliminable Self-Constraint). Positive valence is the interior of movement toward higher coherence. Negative valence is the interior of movement toward lower coherence. This is not metaphor; it is the identity claim applied to affective experience.

This foundational account reframes emotion entirely. Emotions are not separate from cognition, added to perception, or layered onto an otherwise neutral information-processing system. They are the felt registration of the system's coherence dynamics — the way the system experiences its own regulatory state from the inside.

Damasio's (1999) somatic marker hypothesis approaches this insight from the neuroscience side: emotions mark options and outcomes with felt significance that guides decision-making, and patients who lose access to somatic markers (as in ventromedial prefrontal damage) do not become more rational — they become paralyzed, unable to navigate even simple choices. The somatic marker is, in CU terms, a locally accessible valence signal — a felt indication of whether a given option ascends or descends the coherence gradient. Without it, the system has no felt basis for choosing, because the gradient is experientially invisible.

Barrett's (2017) theory of constructed emotion offers a complementary perspective. Barrett argues that emotions are not natural kinds triggered by dedicated neural circuits but context-dependent constructions — the brain's best guess about the meaning of interoceptive and exteroceptive signals, shaped by prior experience and cultural categories. CU is compatible with this constructionist view while grounding it structurally: emotions are constructed precisely because they are coherence assessments, and coherence assessment is inherently context-dependent. The same bodily signals may be constructed as anxiety in one context and excitement in another because the coherence implications of those signals differ across contexts. What remains invariant is the function: the system is evaluating its own coherence state and generating a felt summary that guides action.

4.2 Emotion as Coherence Assessment

Each major class of emotion can be understood as a specific coherence assessment — a felt evaluation of a particular kind of coherence challenge.

Anxiety signals looming or actual incoherence. The system detects that its current configuration is unstable, that threats to integration are present or approaching, or that its regulatory capacity may be insufficient for the demands it faces. Anxiety is not irrational fear; it is the felt aspect of coherence drive (CU-Ψ5) in the presence of perceived threat to viability. It becomes pathological not when it occurs but when it occurs disproportionately to actual coherence risk, or when it persists after the risk has been resolved — when the system's threat detection remains calibrated to conditions that no longer obtain.

Sadness signals loss or depletion that requires reorganization. Something that contributed to the system's coherence — a relationship, a role, a belief, a capacity — has been lost. The felt quality of sadness reflects the system's recognition that its current coherence configuration is no longer viable and must be revised. Grief is extended sadness in response to losses that require deep structural reorganization — the death of a loved one, the end of a relationship, the collapse of a life project. The magnitude of grief correlates with the depth of the coherence restructuring required.

Anger signals boundary violations that disrupt relational or identity coherence. The system detects that something external is actively threatening its integration — overriding its agency, violating its commitments, or imposing incoherence upon it. Anger is directional in a way that anxiety is not: it identifies a source and motivates action toward that source. In coherence terms, anger is the felt aspect of the system's attempt to restore coherence by modifying the external condition that is disrupting it, rather than by modifying its own configuration.

Joy and interest signal successful integration and exploratory opportunity. The system detects that its coherence is increasing — that it is moving up the gradient, that things are coming together, that new possibilities for integration are available. Interest, in particular, is the felt aspect of a coherence gradient that the system can follow: the perception that exploration in a particular direction will yield increased integration. This is why interest is so closely linked to learning, creativity, and meaning — each involves the detection of navigable coherence gradients.

Shame signals that the self-model has been exposed as incoherent in a social context. The system detects a gap between how it presents itself and what it has done, between its identity commitments and its behavior, and this gap has become visible to others. Shame is among the most psychologically devastating emotions because it threatens coherence at the intersection of identity and social embedding — the two domains whose coherence is most difficult to restore independently.

These are not exhaustive descriptions. They are illustrations of a general principle: emotions are domain-specific coherence assessments that provide the system with felt information about the state of its integration. They are not propositional judgments (though they can inform judgment). They are global summaries of system-level alignment, delivered in the currency of valence.

4.3 Motivation as Gradient Navigation

If emotion tells the system how its coherence is doing, motivation governs what the system does about it. Motivation is the felt impulse to move along coherence gradients — to restore, preserve, or expand integration across relevant domains and timescales.

This is the psychological expression of CU-D4 (Gradient Navigation Under Constraint). The system does not compute optimal solutions and then execute them. It follows the local coherence gradient — it moves in the direction that feels like improvement, given its current configuration. Motivation is the experiential name for this gradient-following.

This reframing resolves a longstanding tension in motivation theory. Drive-reduction theories (Hull, 1943) proposed that organisms are motivated to reduce internal tension. Incentive theories proposed that organisms are pulled toward external rewards. Self-determination theory (Deci & Ryan, 2000) proposed that three basic needs — autonomy, competence, and relatedness — ground intrinsic motivation. Each captures part of the picture, but none provides a unifying account.

CU provides the unification. Drive reduction is gradient ascent when coherence has been disrupted — the system moves to restore integration. Incentive motivation is gradient ascent toward perceived coherence gains — the system moves toward configurations that promise greater integration. Deci and Ryan's three needs map directly onto coherence requirements: autonomy is the requirement that the system's actions be coherent with its own identity and values (CU-I4, Self-Referential Constraint Enforcement); competence is the requirement that the system's models effectively track environmental regularities (Rung 17, Predictive Coherence); relatedness is the requirement that interpersonal coherence be maintained (Rungs 22–23, Shared Representations and Coordination Dynamics). These are not three separate needs but three dimensions of the coherence landscape along which the system navigates.

Hunger motivates action to restore physiological coherence. Curiosity motivates exploration to restore cognitive coherence — to fill gaps in the system's model where the gradient is steepest. Loneliness motivates social reconnection to restore interpersonal coherence. Meaning-seeking motivates narrative integration when identity coherence has been threatened at the longest horizons. In each case, the mechanism is the same: the system detects a coherence deficit and moves along the available gradient.

4.4 Why Emotion Suppression Fails

This framework explains a clinical observation that is otherwise puzzling: attempts to suppress emotion typically fail and often make things worse.

If emotions were noise — random perturbations that interfere with rational processing — then suppression should improve functioning. But emotions are not noise. They are regulatory signals carrying information about unresolved coherence conflicts. Suppressing the signal does not resolve the conflict; it merely prevents the system from accessing information it needs to navigate.

Gross's (2002) process model of emotion regulation distinguishes between strategies that modify the emotion-generating situation and strategies that modify the emotional response itself. CU explains why this distinction matters: situation modification addresses the coherence challenge directly (it changes the system's position in H), while response modification suppresses the signal without changing the position. The underlying distortion D(u) remains; the system simply loses access to its felt assessment of that distortion.

Chronic emotional suppression therefore produces a characteristic pattern: the surface appears calm while underlying coherence degrades. The system accumulates unresolved conflicts, unmourned losses, and unaddressed threats. IES (Inverse Entropic Stress; CU-Ψ4) rises because coherence demands continue to accumulate while regulatory capacity is actively being constrained. Eventually, the suppressed material erupts — as panic, breakdown, psychosomatic symptoms, or relational crisis — when the system can no longer contain the distortion.

This is also why emotional numbing in trauma (Section 7) is both protective and costly. Numbing reduces the felt intensity of the coherence crisis, allowing short-term survival. But it also disables the regulatory signals that would guide reintegration, trapping the system in a state of low felt distress and low integrative capacity — the subjective experience of being alive but not living.

4.5 Motivational Pathologies as Coherence Failures

The coherence account of motivation clarifies the structure of motivational pathologies, revealing them as specific configurations in the coherence landscape rather than discrete disorders.

Anxiety disorders reflect hyper-sensitivity to incoherence. Coherence drive (CU-Ψ5) is elevated — the system registers threats to integration with high sensitivity — while regulatory capacity is insufficient to resolve them. The system is perpetually detecting coherence gradients it cannot ascend, producing the characteristic phenomenology of restless, unresolvable distress. Generalized anxiety corresponds to elevated sensitivity across multiple dimensions of M (meaning space); phobic anxiety corresponds to extreme sensitivity along a single dimension; social anxiety corresponds to elevated sensitivity specifically in the social-coherence domain (Rungs 22–23).

Depression reflects a different failure: motivational collapse in the presence of intact coherence drive. The system continues to register that something is wrong — that its configuration is suboptimal, that meaning has been lost, that integration has failed — but perceives no viable gradient. Every direction appears flat or descending. In formal terms, the system is trapped in a local minimum of C(u): a configuration that is locally stable (no nearby state is better) but globally suboptimal (much higher coherence is possible but inaccessible from the current position). The felt quality is not absence of caring but the paralysis of caring without a navigable path — which is why depression so often coexists with intense internal suffering rather than indifference.

This account explains why depression is so often triggered by loss of meaning rather than loss of pleasure. Anhedonia — the inability to experience pleasure — is a real feature of depression, but it is downstream of the more fundamental problem: the collapse of meaning-level coherence (Rung 21). When the long-horizon coherence structure that organizes values, identity, and future orientation disintegrates, the shorter-horizon gradients that pleasure normally provides lose their significance. Activities that once felt rewarding feel empty because the coherence framework within which they were rewarding has collapsed.

Addiction exemplifies the local coherence trap described by CU-Ψ6 at its most destructive. The addictive substance or behavior provides rapid, reliable local coherence restoration — it reduces anxiety, elevates mood, resolves ambiguity, or produces a sense of agency. In the immediate term, it ascends the coherence gradient steeply. But it does so along a dimension that progressively degrades global coherence: physiological regulation deteriorates, relationships erode, identity fragments, and the system becomes increasingly dependent on a single, narrowing strategy for coherence maintenance. The dopaminergic system — which, as Appendix C develops, functions as a coherence-gradient sensitizer — is recruited into ever-more-exclusive service of the local strategy, reducing the system's sensitivity to other coherence gradients and making alternative paths increasingly invisible.

This is why addiction is so difficult to overcome through willpower alone. The addicted system is not failing to choose well; it is navigating a coherence landscape that has been progressively reshaped so that the addictive behavior occupies the deepest accessible basin of attraction. Recovery requires not merely resisting the pull of that basin but restructuring the landscape itself — rebuilding alternative coherence pathways that are deep and rewarding enough to compete. This is the structural rationale for therapeutic approaches that emphasize community, meaning, identity reconstruction, and environmental change rather than simple abstinence.

4.6 Multi-Timescale Coherence Signaling

Emotion and motivation operate across multiple timescales, and much of psychological difficulty arises from conflicts between signals at different horizons.

Some emotional signals prompt immediate corrective action: the startle response, the flush of anger, the pang of hunger. These reflect short-horizon coherence assessments — the system detecting a local threat or opportunity and mobilizing a rapid response.

Other signals reflect longer-horizon coherence concerns: the nagging sense that something in a relationship is wrong, the background unease of living out of alignment with one's values, the growing emptiness when meaningful work is absent. These are not acute but persistent, and they often cannot be resolved by immediate action because the coherence challenge they track spans months, years, or the arc of a life.

The tension between short-horizon and long-horizon signals is structurally identical to the local—global tension formalized in CU-Ψ6, but experienced through the currency of affect. Avoiding a difficult conversation may reduce anxiety now (short-horizon coherence gain) while eroding relational trust (long-horizon coherence loss). Staying in a secure but unfulfilling career preserves financial and social stability (medium-horizon) while progressively degrading meaning (longest-horizon).

Psychological growth often consists in learning to tolerate short-term negative valence in service of long-term coherence gain — to endure the discomfort of a difficult conversation because relational integrity matters more than momentary ease. This capacity is not willpower in the folk sense. It is the system's ability to weigh gradients at multiple timescales simultaneously and to follow the longer-horizon gradient even when it conflicts with the shorter one. It requires, in formal terms, that the system's effective coherence functional C(u) weight long-horizon integration more heavily than short-horizon relief — a capacity that develops gradually and can be damaged by trauma, never-resolved stress, or environments that reward only short-horizon optimization.

This is why meaning plays such a powerful motivational role. Meaning is not an abstract luxury layered onto basic drives. It is the longest-horizon coherence signal — the felt assessment of whether values, identity, and future orientation are integrated into a sustainable structure (Rung 21). When meaning collapses, motivation collapses with it, even in the absence of immediate threat or deprivation, because the longest-horizon gradient has gone flat. Viktor Frankl's (1946) observation — that humans can endure almost any suffering if they perceive it as meaningful — is, in CU terms, a statement about the motivational primacy of long-horizon coherence: a system that maintains meaning can tolerate enormous short-horizon distortion because the longest gradient remains navigable.

The relationship between short-horizon and long-horizon coherence signals described here instantiates a well-established principle in dynamical systems theory: Haken's slaving principle, in which the slow modes of a system's dynamics constrain and organize its fast modes (Haken, 1983). Identity commitments, values, and meaning structures change on timescales of months to decades; perceptual updates, emotional reactions, and behavioral impulses change on timescales of milliseconds to hours. The slow variables do not merely coexist with the fast ones — they set the landscape within which fast dynamics unfold. This is why a shift in core meaning (a slow variable) can reorganize an entire pattern of perception and behavior, while thousands of perceptual updates leave identity untouched. It is also why ego dissolution and identity crises feel catastrophic: when the slow variables destabilize, the fast dynamics lose their organizing constraints and the system enters a transient state of high entropy before settling into a new configuration — or failing to.

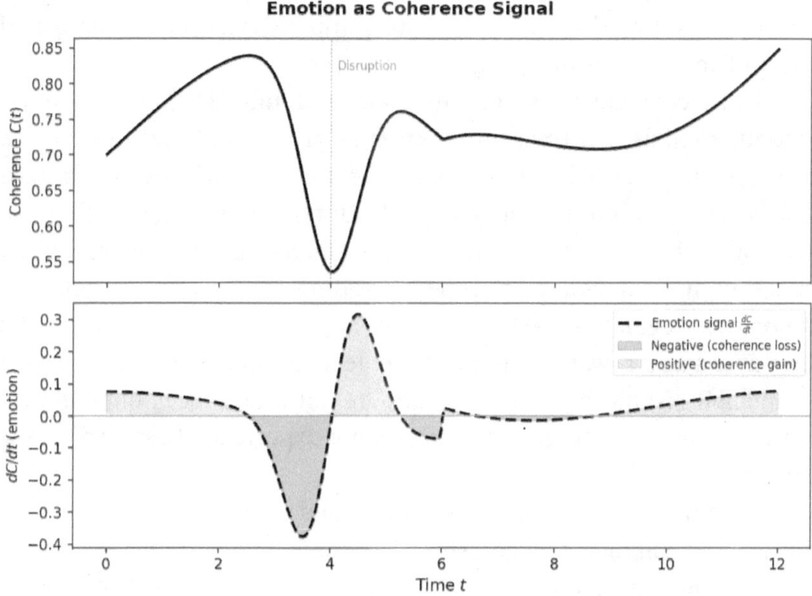

Figure 4. *Emotion as coherence signal. The solid line tracks coherence C(t) across time as the system encounters a minor stressor, a major disruption, and a recovery phase. The dashed line shows the corresponding emotional signal — a derivative-like readout that registers both the rate and direction of coherence change. Negative emotion signals coherence loss; positive emotion signals coherence restoration. The framework treats affect not as noise to be managed but as the primary information channel for coherence assessment.*

4.7 The Indispensability of Affect

Emotion and motivation are not optional features of psychological systems. They are not luxuries that evolution added to an otherwise functional cognitive architecture. They are the system's primary mode of access to its own coherence dynamics — the felt summary of where it stands, where it is heading, and what needs to change.

Attempts to model human behavior without affect inevitably reintroduce it under different names — preferences, utilities, reward functions, incentive saliences — stripped of their experiential and regulatory significance. These substitutes preserve the formal structure (the system has a gradient and follows it) while discarding the phenomenology (the system feels the gradient and acts from within that feeling). CU insists that the phenomenology is not decorative. It is constitutive. Valence is not a readout of underlying computational processes; it is the interior of those processes, as CU-C3 specifies.

This has consequences for any field that models human behavior. Economic models that treat preferences as given and fixed miss the fact that preferences are dynamic coherence assessments that shift as the system's configuration changes. Behavioral nudge approaches that manipulate choice architecture without attending to coherence may produce compliant behavior while degrading the system's capacity for autonomous regulation. AI alignment approaches that model human values as a static reward function to be learned and maximized miss the fundamental insight that human values are not preferences but coherence constraints, and that their satisfaction is not experienced as reward but as meaning.

This section has reframed emotion and motivation as coherence signals — regulatory mechanisms that track the system's position in meaning space and generate gradients toward integration. Emotions are not noise to be suppressed or data to be processed but structural indicators of coherence state. Motivation is the psychological expression of coherence drive (CU-Ψ5): the inherent directedness of the system toward greater integration.

Section 5: Identity, Personality, and the Self — Coherence Across the Person

If perception, cognition, and memory regulate coherence within the moment, and emotion and motivation signal the state of that regulation, then identity and personality regulate coherence across the lifespan. They are not optional features layered onto a functioning mind. They are the structures that allow psychological systems to remain intelligible to themselves across time — to act coherently not just now but over the arc of a life.

The Consciousness paper developed the most extensive formal treatment of identity in the CU series: the five identity conditions (CU-I1 through CU-I5), the foundational principle of identity as constraint-preserved coherence (CU-FP8 and sub-principles CU-FP8a through CU-FP8e), and the demonstration that identity is the precondition for consciousness because consciousness arises when identity-maintenance requires a unified, valence-bearing perspective. This section translates that formal apparatus into the psychological domain, showing how identity, personality, and the self function as long-horizon coherence structures that are continuously maintained, defended, and — in healthy development — revised.

5.1 Identity as Long-Horizon Coherence Structure

Identity, in the CU framework, is not a static essence, a narrative fiction, or a social construction. It is a long-horizon coherence structure: a relatively stable pattern that integrates values, memories, roles, commitments, and self-understanding into a form capable of guiding action across extended temporal horizons.

This follows directly from CU-FP8 (Identity as Constraint-Preserved Coherence): a system has identity when it persists through change by preserving self-enforcing viability constraints. In the psychological domain, the viability constraints that define identity are not metabolic but organizational — they are the commitments, values, self-understandings, and relational bonds that make a person this person rather than some other. When these constraints are preserved through change, identity persists. When they collapse, identity is lost — not in the sense of physical death but in the psychologically devastating sense of no longer knowing who one is.

Each of the five identity conditions maps onto psychological reality:

CU-I1 (Viability Constraint Condition) requires that there exist states the system must not enter without ceasing to exist as that system. Psychologically, these are the commitments and values so central to self-understanding that their violation or abandonment would constitute an identity crisis. The parent who discovers she is capable of abandoning her child; the person of integrity who catches himself in a fundamental dishonesty; the believer who confronts the collapse of her faith — each faces the boundary of V, the region beyond which this self cannot persist.

CU-I2 (Constraint Persistence Across Substrate Change) requires that identity-defining constraints persist even when components are replaced. Psychologically, this explains how identity survives enormous transformation. A person can change careers, move countries, end marriages, recover from addiction, undergo religious conversion — and remain the same person, provided the deepest organizing constraints persist through the change. The pattern that makes someone herself is not any particular role, relationship, or belief but the organizational structure that connects them.

CU-I3 (Irreversible Path-Dependence) requires that history constrains the future in ways that cannot be fully undone. Psychologically, this is the reality that experience is indelible. Trauma reshapes the constraints under which the system operates — not merely by depositing memories but by altering the landscape of what is possible, what feels safe, and what can be integrated (Section 7). Development proceeds irreversibly: the adolescent cannot return to childhood innocence; the parent cannot unknow what parenthood teaches. This irreversibility is what generates genuine psychological stakes.

CU-I4 (Self-Referential Constraint Enforcement) requires that the system itself participate in enforcing its identity-defining constraints. Psychologically, this is the distinction between authentic identity and externally imposed role. A person whose identity is entirely maintained by social scaffolding — who is coherent only because her environment never challenges her — has borrowed identity, not genuine identity. Authentic identity requires self-enforcement: the person must actively maintain her commitments, values, and self-understanding, even when the environment does not reinforce them. This is what Deci and Ryan

(2000) call autonomy: not independence from social context but self-endorsement of the constraints that organize one's life.

CU-I5 (Identity Collapse Thresholds) requires that there exist critical thresholds beyond which recovery is impossible for that system. Psychologically, this means that some experiences, some revelations, and some betrayals genuinely destroy the self that existed before them. The person who emerges from a shattering trauma is not the person who entered it, even if she remembers being that person. Some losses cannot be recovered; some transformations are one-way. This is what gives identity its weight and makes identity-level coherence maintenance so consequential.

5.1.1 Identity as Constraint-Structure Persistence

The five identity conditions converge on a structural definition that can now be stated precisely: identity is the persistence of a system's constraint structure across time. This goes beyond the claim that identity involves continuity of memory or narrative. Section 3.3.1 established that memory is best understood not as stored information but as the accumulated deformation of the system's viable future trajectories — the goals that survived conflict, the boundaries discovered through failure, the interpretive patterns shaped by experience. Identity, then, is not the sum of what the system remembers; it is the persistence of the navigational structure that memory has shaped.

Let K represent the system's constraint state at any given time — the totality of commitments, values, skills, relational bonds, threat calibrations, and interpretive frameworks that together determine which futures the system treats as admissible. Identity persists when K changes only through small, continuous deformation — when the system learns, grows, and adapts without discontinuous rupture of its organizing structure. Identity breaks when K undergoes a large, sudden restructuring — when the constraint manifold is reorganized so drastically that the system's prior navigational structure no longer applies.

This yields a taxonomy of identity change that maps onto psychological experience with considerable precision:

Learning and ordinary development involve small constraint deformation. The system acquires new skills, updates beliefs, and adjusts expectations while preserving its overall organizing structure. The person remains recognizably herself. Identity is maintained smoothly.

Major life transitions. Adolescence, career change, religious conversion, parenthood — involve moderate restructuring with coherent continuity. The constraint manifold is substantially reorganized, but the process is gradual enough and internally connected enough that the person experiences transformation rather than rupture. She can narrate how she became who she now is.

Trauma involves large, discontinuous constraint restructuring (Section 6). The event forces a rapid reorganization of the system's navigational structure — a regime shift in which the landscape of admissible futures changes abruptly. The person often reports feeling that she is "not the same person," yet identity persists in attenuated form because core constraint structures survive the transition. Trauma is a regime shift, not an identity break.

Identity fracture. Severe dissociation, prolonged personality change under extreme conditions — involves reorganization so extensive that the prior constraint manifold is largely replaced. The substrate persists; the organizing structure does not. The person occupies a borderline zone between same-agent and different-agent.

Identity death. Advanced neurodegeneration, catastrophic psychotic break without recovery — involves the loss of constraint continuity altogether. The system may continue to function biologically, but the navigational structure that made it this person has been destroyed. What remains is a system, not this system.

This taxonomy is not merely descriptive. It provides the structural bridge between the formal identity conditions (CU-I1 through CU-I5) and the clinical phenomena of Section 6. Trauma, pathology, and therapeutic recovery all involve movements along this continuum — and understanding where a person stands within it determines what kind of intervention their situation requires.

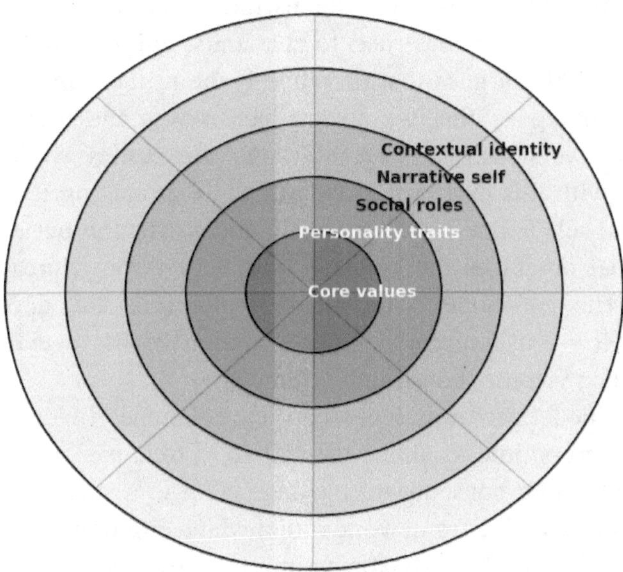

Figure 5. Identity as nested coherence structure. Concentric rings represent layers of identity integration, from core values at the center through personality traits, social roles, narrative self, and contextual identity. Radial connections represent integration across layers. Identity coherence requires not uniformity but structural alignment: each layer must be compatible with the others under the constraints of lived experience.

5.2 The Self-Model

Psychological coherence at the level of identity requires a self-model — a compressed internal representation of who the system is, what it values, what it can do, and how it relates to its environment and its history. This self-model need not be explicit or verbal, but it must support continuity: the sense that past actions, present choices, and future consequences belong to the same agent.

The self-model is the psychological instantiation of CU-I4 (Self-Referential Constraint Enforcement). It is the structure through which the system monitors and maintains its own identity-defining constraints. Without it, there is no locus from which identity can be enforced, and the system's coherence is entirely dependent on external scaffolding.

McAdams (2001) describes the narrative self as the internalized, evolving story a person constructs to give unity, purpose, and meaning to life. Bruner (1990) argues that narrative is the primary mode of human self-understanding — that we do not have selves and then tell stories about them; we construct selves through the stories we tell. CU is compatible with this narrative emphasis while grounding it structurally: the narrative self is not merely a cognitive construction but a coherence structure that organizes the system's trajectory through meaning space (CU-Ψ1). The self-model is the meaning map (CU-Ψ2) applied to the agent herself — a compressed representation of the agent's position, trajectory, and viability constraints within M.

The self-model performs several critical coherence functions. It binds experience across time, enabling the system to treat past actions, present choices, and future consequences as belonging to a single trajectory. It provides the evaluative framework within which emotions are interpreted — shame, pride, guilt, and satisfaction are all assessments of the self relative to its own standards, requiring a self-model against which assessment can occur. It supports agency by enabling the system to predict the consequences of its own actions and to select actions coherent with its values and commitments. And it grounds moral responsibility: without a self-model that connects past actions to present identity, neither guilt nor growth is possible.

Crucially, the self-model cannot fully represent the system whose model it is — a constraint that the epistemic principle CU-Ep4 (Bounded Reflection) identifies as structurally necessary. Self-knowledge is always partial, because the regulatory processes that construct and maintain the self-model are themselves part of the system being modeled. This bounded character of reflection is not a defect but a structural feature of any system complex enough to represent itself.

5.3 Personality as Stable Coherence Strategy

Personality traits can be understood as stable coherence strategies — characteristic ways of navigating the coherence landscape that have been shaped by developmental experience, temperament, and environmental feedback.

The Big Five model (Costa & McCrae, 1992) identifies five broad trait dimensions: openness, conscientiousness, extraversion, agreeableness, and neuroticism. From a CU perspective, each reflects a different regulatory emphasis within the coherence landscape:

Conscientiousness prioritizes coherence through order, predictability, and planful constraint. Highly conscientious systems reduce uncertainty by imposing structure, maintaining routines, and adhering to rules. This strategy excels in environments that reward reliability and long-term planning. It becomes maladaptive when rigidity prevents accommodation to changed circumstances — when the system cannot reorganize its coherence strategy even when the old strategy no longer works.

Openness prioritizes coherence through exploration, flexibility, and receptivity to novel configurations. Highly open systems maintain coherence by expanding their integrative capacity rather than constraining their inputs. This strategy excels in environments that reward creativity, adaptation, and tolerance of ambiguity. It becomes maladaptive when the system's appetite for novelty overwhelms its capacity for integration, producing fragmentation rather than expanded coherence.

Extraversion prioritizes coherence through social engagement and distributed regulation. Highly extraverted systems maintain coherence partly through interpersonal feedback — they regulate by connecting. This reflects the Ladder's insight (Rungs 22–23) that coherence can be distributed across agents. The strategy becomes maladaptive when social dependency substitutes for internal regulation — when the system cannot maintain coherence without external input.

Agreeableness prioritizes interpersonal coherence — the maintenance of harmonious social fields. Highly agreeable systems invest regulatory resources in preserving relational alignment. This strategy supports collective coherence but becomes maladaptive when it systematically subordinates the system's own coherence needs to others', producing resentment, burnout, or self-erasure.

Neuroticism reflects elevated sensitivity to coherence threat. Highly neurotic systems detect incoherence earlier, react more strongly to perturbation, and mobilize regulatory resources at lower thresholds. This is the trait most directly connected to CU-Ψ5 (Psychological Coherence

Drive) — specifically, to the intensity of the system's threat-detection sensitivity. In moderate form, it supports vigilance and preparedness. In extreme form, it overwhelms regulatory capacity, producing chronic anxiety, rumination, and difficulty recovering from perturbation.

This reframing dissolves a persistent confusion in personality psychology. Traits are often treated as causes of behavior — as if conscientiousness makes a person organize her desk, or neuroticism makes a person anxious. From a coherence standpoint, traits are better understood as patterns of regulation that have historically maintained coherence for that system in that environment. They persist because they work — because they have, over the system's developmental history, succeeded in maintaining integration under the specific conditions the system has faced. This is why traits are relatively stable but not immutable: they reflect deep attractor structures (Appendix F) that can be reshaped through sustained reorganization but resist casual perturbation.

Mischel's (1968) critique of trait theory — his demonstration that behavior varies dramatically across situations — is not a refutation of traits but an illustration of CU-Ψ6. Local coherence demands vary across contexts, and the system adapts its regulatory strategy accordingly. What remains stable is not the behavior but the coherence strategy — the characteristic way the system navigates the tradeoff between local and global integration.

5.4 Identity Coherence Is Not Consistency

A critical distinction: identity coherence is not synonymous with consistency. Healthy identities accommodate contradiction, growth, and revision. What matters is not sameness across time but integratability — the capacity to incorporate new experience into an existing coherence structure without shattering it.

This follows from the distinction between rigidity and coherence developed in Section 2.4. A rigid identity maintains consistency by refusing new input — by filtering perception, distorting memory, and avoiding experiences that would require revision. A coherent identity maintains integration by absorbing new input — by revising the self-model when experience demands it, extending the narrative to accommodate contradiction, and expanding the viability region V rather than contracting it.

Kegan's (1982) constructive-developmental theory describes this process as a sequence of increasingly complex meaning-making structures, each capable of holding more contradiction and ambiguity than the last. Erikson's (1968) psychosocial stages trace the progressive expansion of integrative demands — from trust versus mistrust in infancy, through identity versus role confusion in adolescence, to integrity versus despair in old age. Both theories describe, in different vocabularies, what CU formalizes as the expansion of coherence capacity across development.

The CU contribution is to specify the structural mechanism. Development does not merely add complexity; it shifts the system's deepest attractor from external regulation toward internal coherence (Appendix F). The infant's identity is maintained entirely by external scaffolding (caregivers, routines, physical contact). The child's identity is maintained partly by social approval — belonging, imitation, and conformity serve as the primary coherence strategy. The adolescent must renegotiate identity as bodily, social, and moral demands shift simultaneously, and the coherence strategy that served childhood (conform, belong, imitate) no longer suffices. The mature adult maintains identity through internal coherence structures that can withstand social pressure, accommodate contradiction, and revise themselves without collapsing.

This developmental trajectory is not inevitable. Many adults stabilize at coherence strategies characteristic of earlier developmental profiles — strategies organized around social approval, self-image maintenance, or rigid ideological commitment. These strategies are not pathological per se; they are viable under conditions that do not demand deeper integration. They become pathological when the environment shifts and the system cannot adapt — when the strategy that once maintained coherence now produces escalating incoherence.

5.5 Self-Deception as Coherence Defense (CU-Ψ11)

Self-deception is among the most psychologically and morally consequential phenomena that CU illuminates. It can be precisely characterized in the formal framework:

CU-Ψ11. Self-Deception as Meaning-Map Distortion. Self-deception occurs when the system's meaning map Φ is distorted to preserve local coherence — specifically, identity coherence — at the expense of global integrability. The distorted map Φ′ avoids regions of meaning space M that contain truths incompatible with the current self-model, ensuring that destabilizing information never reaches the system's integrative processes.

Self-deception is a local coherence defense. In the short term, it stabilizes the system by preventing intolerable conflict between self-understanding and reality. The person who cannot face the failure of his marriage maintains coherence by reinterpreting evidence, minimizing concerns, or attributing problems to external causes. The professional who cannot acknowledge her incompetence maintains coherence by blaming circumstances, avoiding feedback, or surrounding herself with people who confirm her self-assessment. In each case, the meaning map is adjusted so that the threatening truth falls outside the region of M that the system navigates.

The cost is cumulative. Each act of self-deception increases the distortion D(u) of the system's configuration — the gap between the map and the territory grows. The system must exert increasing regulatory effort to maintain the distorted map against the pressure of accumulating evidence. IES (CU-Ψ4) rises because coherence demands (maintain the story) escalate while the territory the map must exclude expands. Eventually, the distortion becomes unsustainable: reality breaks through, or the system's regulatory capacity is exhausted, or the distorted map produces actions so misaligned with reality that their consequences are undeniable.

This is why self-deception often feels protective yet leads to cumulative breakdown. It is the identity-level analogue of the local—global coherence tension (CU-Ψ6): the system gains local coherence (the self-model is preserved) at the cost of global coherence (the map increasingly diverges from the territory).

From this perspective, many moral and psychological failures are not best explained by ignorance or malice but by identity-level coherence preservation under threat. People rationalize, deny, and externalize not because they lack information but because certain truths cannot be integrated without destabilizing their self-model — without pushing the system toward or across the boundary of V. This structural account of rationalization connects directly to the Anti-Rationalization principle (CU-L6), which identifies the systematic distortion of reasoning in service of coherence preservation, and to CU-E-5 (Self-Deception as Ethical Failure), which holds that self-deception is not merely a psychological phenomenon but a structural precondition for moral failure. This is not an excuse; it is a structural explanation that has direct implications for how moral failure should be understood and addressed. The ethical analysis developed in CU — Ethics takes up this insight in detail.

5.6 The Social Constitution of Identity

Identity coherence is not constructed or maintained in isolation. Self-models are shaped, stabilized, and challenged through relationships, roles, and shared narratives. Social feedback provides continuous information about whether the self the system projects is coherent with the self others perceive. Roles provide pre-structured coherence scaffolding — templates for organizing behavior, values, and self-understanding that reduce the burden of individual construction.

This social dimension connects identity to the Ladder's social rungs. Shared representations (Rung 22) provide the symbolic resources — language, categories, cultural narratives — within which self-models are constructed. Coordination dynamics (Rung 23) provide the relational feedback through which self-models are tested and refined. Norm formation (Rung 24) provides the evaluative framework within which self-models are judged adequate or inadequate. Identity is therefore not merely an individual achievement but a joint production of individual regulation and social scaffolding.

Cooley's (1902) looking-glass self and Mead's (1934) symbolic interactionism capture this social constitution: the self arises through the internalization of others' responses. CU grounds this sociological insight structurally: the self-model is partly maintained through distributed coherence — the system outsources some of its identity-enforcement to social processes (Rung 22–24). This outsourcing is functionally necessary in early development (when internal regulation is insufficient) and remains important throughout life. But it introduces vulnerability: when social environments reward rigidity, conformity, or domination, identity coherence may be preserved at the cost of empathy, adaptability, and epistemic integrity.

The system's deepest attractor (Appendix F) determines how much identity coherence depends on social scaffolding versus internal regulation. Systems organized around social-approval attractors (Profile 2) are most vulnerable to social manipulation because their identity coherence is most dependent on external validation. Systems organized around epistemic coherence attractors (Profile 4) are most resistant to social pressure but may sacrifice relational connection. The integrated profile (Profile 5) achieves identity coherence that is both internally grounded and relationally responsive — stable under social pressure without being isolated from social reality.

5.7 Failures of Identity Coherence

Failures of identity coherence produce distinctive forms of suffering, each locatable within the formal framework.

Identity diffusion — the chronic inability to consolidate a stable self-model — reflects a state in which the system has no deep attractor. Multiple possible configurations compete without resolution; the system oscillates between partial identities without integrating them. In formal terms, the coherence landscape around identity has no dominant basin of attraction — only shallow, competing minima that the system moves between without settling.

Chronic shame reflects persistent detection of a gap between the self-model and the self's actual configuration — particularly as socially perceived. The system cannot close the gap because closing it would require either revising the self-model (threatening identity coherence) or changing the behavior (threatening other coherence commitments). Shame persists because the coherence conflict is structural, not merely informational.

Impostor syndrome reflects a specific form of meaning-map distortion in which evidence of competence cannot be integrated into the self-model. The system maintains a self-model organized around inadequacy while accumulating contradictory evidence. The evidence is processed but not incorporated — it is deflected by attributions to luck, timing, or deception of others. This is self-deception in reverse: instead of distorting the map to preserve a flattering self-image, the system distorts the map to preserve an unflattering one, because the unflattering image has become the deeper attractor.

Existential anxiety reflects the detection of a threat not to any particular identity commitment but to the coherence of the identity structure itself — the felt recognition that the self-model may be fundamentally inadequate, that the story may not hold, that the meaning one has constructed may not survive scrutiny. Existential anxiety is coherence drive (CU-Ψ5) operating at the deepest level: the system is registering a threat to V itself, not merely to its position within V.

5.8 Maturity as Expanded Integrative Capacity

Psychological maturity, seen through this lens, is not the elimination of conflict but the expansion of integrative capacity. The mature person is not someone who has resolved all contradictions or achieved a final, stable identity. She is someone whose coherence structure can hold more tension without fragmenting, revise more deeply without collapsing, and act coherently across more complex moral and social landscapes.

This is what Appendix F formalizes as the progression from externally regulated to internally integrated attractor profiles. The direction of maturity is toward deeper, more internally grounded coherence attractors that can stabilize the system without requiring the world to remain simple. The most mature systems — those operating from the integrated coherence profile (Profile 5) — coordinate epistemic integrity with relational attunement, holding truth and compassion together rather than sacrificing one for the other.

This trajectory is not guaranteed. Development can arrest, regress, or be blocked by insufficient environmental support. Trauma can force the system back to earlier attractor profiles. Social environments that punish individuation or reward conformity can suppress the transitions that maturity requires. What CU adds to developmental psychology is the structural specification of what these transitions involve: not the acquisition of new information or the learning of new skills, but the reorganization of the coherence landscape around deeper, more internally regulated attractors.

This section has analyzed identity as constraint-preserved coherence across developmental time — not a static core self but a dynamic attractor structure that persists through change. Personality traits are stable patterns of coherence navigation, and the self is the system's recursive model of its own coherence dynamics. Development follows attractor dynamics, with the capacity for growth depending on both internal resources and environmental coherence support.

Section 6: Sexuality, Attachment, and Intimacy — Interpersonal Coherence

Sexuality, attachment, and intimacy are often treated as special domains in psychology — areas where rational explanation gives way to instinct, culture, or moral controversy, and where theory becomes tentative or ideologically charged. From the perspective of Coherence Universalism, this exceptionalism is unnecessary. These domains are best understood as mechanisms of interpersonal coherence: the processes through which psychological systems extend, distribute, and negotiate coherence across the boundary between self and other.

This section occupies a transitional position in the paper's architecture. The preceding sections treated coherence as an individual achievement — something a single system maintains within itself. But human psychology is not solitary. The Coherence Ladder establishes that coherence becomes distributed across agents beginning at Rung 22 (Shared Representations) and extending through Rungs 23–26 (Coordination Dynamics, Norm Formation, Institutions, Culture). Attachment and intimacy are the earliest and most intense forms of distributed coherence — the dyadic precursors to the group-level shared coherence fields (CU-Ψ12) developed in Section 9.

6.1 Attachment as Distributed Coherence Regulation

Attachment theory, originated by Bowlby (1969) and extended by Ainsworth (1978), Hazan and Shaver (1987), and others, describes one of the most robust findings in developmental psychology: human beings are born into regulatory dependence on caregivers, and the patterns established in that early regulatory relationship shape psychological functioning across the lifespan.

CU provides a structural account of why this is so. Infants cannot maintain physiological or emotional coherence independently. Their nervous systems are not yet capable of the self-referential constraint enforcement (CU-I4) that adult identity requires. They depend on caregivers to provide external regulation — to modulate arousal, restore equilibrium after distress, and scaffold the perceptual and emotional integration that the infant's system cannot yet achieve on its own. In CU terms, the infant's viability region V is not self-maintained; it is jointly maintained by a dyadic system in which the caregiver functions as an external coherence regulator.

This is not a metaphor. The biological evidence is extensive. Caregiver contact regulates infant heart rate, cortisol levels, temperature, and respiratory rhythm (Hofer, 1994). Disruption of the attachment bond produces physiological dysregulation that is measurable and sometimes lasting. The caregiver is, literally, part of the system that maintains the infant's coherence.

This pattern does not disappear in adulthood. It becomes more complex, more reciprocal, and more dependent on representational rather than purely physiological channels — but the fundamental structure persists. Adult intimate relationships function as shared regulatory systems. Partners distribute emotional load, stabilize each other's identity coherence, co-regulate arousal, and extend each other's capacity for coherence maintenance beyond what either could sustain alone. Sbarra and Hazan (2008) describe adult attachment bonds as involving the same regulatory functions Bowlby identified in infant-caregiver pairs: proximity seeking, safe haven, secure base, and separation distress. The phenomenology differs; the structural function — distributed coherence regulation — is continuous.

This explains why relationship loss is so psychologically devastating. The dissolution of an attachment bond does not merely remove a source of pleasure or companionship. It removes part of the system that maintained coherence. The surviving partner must now self-regulate processes that were previously jointly regulated — a sudden and often overwhelming increase in regulatory load. In formal terms, the system's effective viability region V contracts abruptly, because configurations that were viable with distributed support are no longer viable without it. Grief is the felt aspect of this contraction — the system's registration that its coherence landscape has fundamentally changed and that reorganization is required.

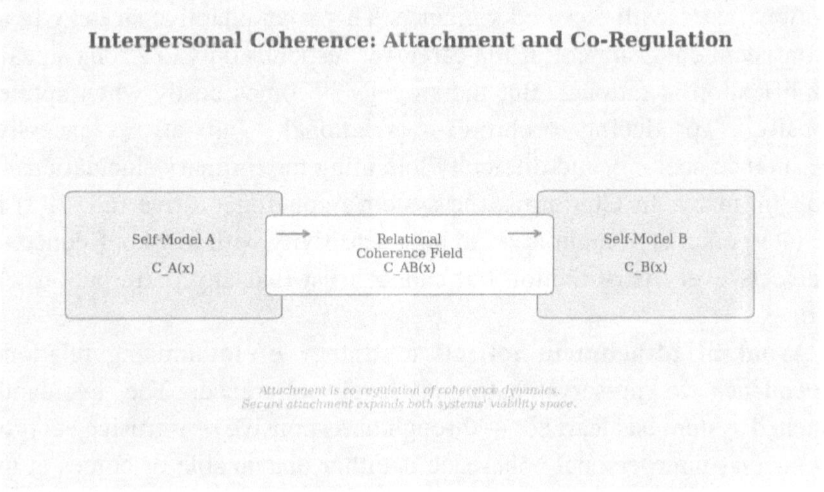

Interpersonal Coherence: Attachment and Co-Regulation

Self-Model A
C_A(x)

Relational
Coherence Field
C_AB(x)

Self-Model B
C_B(x)

Attachment is co-regulation of coherence dynamics.
Secure attachment expands both systems' viability space.

Figure 6. *Attachment styles as coherence regulation strategies. Secure attachment achieves flexible distributed regulation; anxious attachment over-relies on external coherence supply; avoidant restricts to internal regulation; disorganized reflects contradictory demands preventing stable strategy formation.*

6.2 Attachment Styles as Coherence Strategies

Ainsworth's (1978) classification of attachment styles — secure, anxious, and avoidant — can be precisely characterized as learned coherence strategies, each representing an adaptive response to a developmental environment with specific coherence affordances.

Secure attachment reflects confidence that interpersonal coherence can be restored through relational engagement. The securely attached system has learned — through repeated experience of responsive caregiving — that disruptions to shared coherence are temporary and reparable. It can tolerate separation because it trusts that reconnection will occur. It can tolerate distress because it has internalized the regulatory pattern that the caregiver once provided externally. In formal terms, the system has internalized a reliable model of the interpersonal coherence landscape: it knows where the gradients are and trusts that they are navigable.

Anxious attachment reflects heightened sensitivity to interpersonal incoherence, paired with hyperactivation of regulatory signaling. The anxiously attached system has learned — through inconsistent caregiving — that coherence support is available but unreliable. It responds by amplifying distress signals, seeking proximity intensely, and monitoring relational cues with elevated vigilance. This is an adaptive strategy in an inconsistent environment: if the caregiver responds only to strong signals, amplification is rational. But the strategy becomes costly when applied globally, producing chronic relational anxiety, excessive reassurance-seeking, and difficulty tolerating the ordinary fluctuations of adult intimacy. In CU terms, the system's coherence drive (CU-Ψ5) in the interpersonal domain is set to high sensitivity with low confidence — it detects every perturbation but cannot trust that any perturbation will resolve.

Avoidant attachment reflects a strategy of minimizing relational dependence to preserve autonomy-level coherence. The avoidantly attached system has learned — through unresponsive or intrusive caregiving — that interpersonal coherence is either unavailable or comes at the cost of autonomy. It responds by suppressing attachment signaling, maintaining emotional distance, and relying on self-regulation rather than co-regulation. This strategy preserves coherence along the autonomy dimension (CU-I4) but sacrifices it along the interpersonal dimension (Rungs 22–23). The avoidant system maintains a self-enforced viability region that is smaller but more independently sustainable — at the cost of the expanded coherence that intimate connection makes possible.

Disorganized attachment — added by Main and Hesse (1990) — reflects a coherence crisis in which the attachment figure is simultaneously the source of comfort and the source of threat. The system cannot organize a coherent strategy because the two options available (approach for regulation, withdraw from danger) are mutually contradictory. This produces fragmented, contradictory behavior and often underlies severe psychological difficulties in adulthood. In CU terms, the system faces an irresolvable coherence conflict at the most fundamental regulatory level: the gradient that should lead toward safety leads simultaneously toward danger, and no coherent navigation is possible.

These styles are not pathologies in themselves. They are adaptations to developmental environments with different coherence affordances — strategies that made sense given the regulatory landscape the system actually faced. They become sources of difficulty when they persist into environments with different affordances — when the anxious system applies hypervigilance to a reliable partner, or the avoidant system withholds from a responsive one. Therapy in this domain often involves making the implicit coherence strategy explicit and supporting the system's reorganization toward strategies that match current rather than historical conditions.

6.3 Sexuality as Amplified Coherence Dynamics

Sexuality occupies a distinct but related position in the coherence framework. Beyond reproduction or pleasure, sexuality involves heightened vulnerability, mutual attunement, and identity integration. Sexual experience amplifies coherence dynamics — desire, shame, trust, fear, merger, boundary — making it one of the most powerful sites of both regulation and dysregulation in human life.

The amplification occurs because sexual experience engages multiple coherence layers simultaneously. Embodiment, affect, cognition, identity, and social meaning are all activated and all at stake. The body is exposed and responsive. Emotions are intensified by vulnerability. Identity is implicated because sexual experience touches on fundamental questions of agency, desirability, power, and self-worth. Social meaning is engaged because sexuality is never culturally neutral — every sexual encounter occurs within a framework of norms, expectations, and judgments that shape its coherence implications.

When these layers are integrated — when bodily experience, emotional connection, identity coherence, and relational context align — sexual intimacy can deepen coherence in ways that few other experiences can. The phenomenology of sexual connection at its best involves a temporary expansion of the self-model to include the other, a relaxation of defensive boundaries, and a heightened mutual attunement that functions as intensive co-regulation. In CU terms, the dyadic system achieves a shared coherence configuration that is richer than either system's individual capacity — a transient but powerful extension of V through interpersonal integration.

When these layers are fragmented, coerced, or concealed, sexuality destabilizes coherence at multiple levels simultaneously. Sexual trauma, discussed further in Section 7, disrupts embodied regulation, emotional signaling, trust, memory, and identity all at once — producing cascading incoherence that is particularly resistant to reintegration precisely because so many layers are simultaneously affected.

6.4 Coherence Conflicts in Intimacy

Many difficulties in intimate life arise not from pathology but from coherence conflicts across levels — precisely the local—global tension formalized in CU-Ψ6, operating across the domains that intimacy brings into contact.

A person may experience sexual desire that threatens identity coherence. Desire for a partner outside one's committed relationship, desire that conflicts with moral or religious commitments, desire for experiences that one's self-model cannot accommodate — these are not failures of willpower but coherence conflicts in which one dimension of integration (embodied, affective) pulls against another (identity, relational, moral). The distress arises not from the desire itself but from the inability to integrate it without destabilizing coherence elsewhere.

Conversely, relational expectations may suppress desire in ways that preserve surface harmony while eroding authenticity. A person who conforms to a partner's sexual expectations at the cost of her own experience maintains relational coherence by sacrificing embodied and identity-level coherence. The surface appears stable; the underlying FCS (CU-Ψ3) declines as more and more of the system's experience is excluded from the meaning map.

Shame emerges at precisely these fault lines. As described in Section 3.2, shame signals that the self-model has been exposed as incoherent in a socially relevant domain. In sexuality, shame is particularly potent because the exposure is simultaneously embodied, relational, and identity-relevant. Sexual shame often reflects not moral failure but the system's detection of a gap between layers of coherence that cannot be closed within the current meaning-map structure — between what the body wants, what the self-model permits, and what the social context rewards.

6.5 Consent, Agency, and the Coherence Criterion

Coherence Universalism does not prescribe particular sexual norms or relational structures. It does not adjudicate between monogamy and polyamory, between traditional and progressive sexual ethics, or between competing cultural frameworks for understanding gender and desire. These are questions that depend on context, values, and the specific coherence landscapes of the individuals and communities involved.

What CU does provide is a structural criterion for evaluation: do a person's sexual and relational practices support or undermine coherence across the relevant domains and timescales?

This criterion generates several principled distinctions:

Practices that preserve consent support coherence because they ensure that both systems' agency — their capacity for self-referential constraint enforcement (CU-I4) — remains intact. Coercion degrades coherence by overriding one system's regulatory autonomy, forcing it into configurations that are not self-endorsed. The damage is not merely to the coerced party's preferences but to her identity-level coherence: the capacity to experience herself as the agent of her own life has been violated.

Practices that support integratability — that allow experience to be incorporated into the self-model and relational narrative without excessive distortion — tend to support coherence over time. Practices that require concealment, compartmentalization, or systematic self-deception tend to degrade it, even when they provide short-term pleasure or relief, because they increase the gap between the meaning map and the territory (CU-Ψ11).

Practices that distribute regulatory benefit — that enhance both partners' coherence rather than enhancing one at the expense of the other — tend toward sustainable intimacy. Relationships organized around asymmetric extraction — where one partner's coherence is systematically maintained by depleting the other's — tend toward instability or covert damage, even when the surface appears functional.

These distinctions do not resolve every ethical question about sexuality and intimacy, but they provide a non-arbitrary framework for evaluation that does not depend on appeals to tradition, nature, or cultural consensus. The criterion is structural: does this practice, in this context, support or undermine the coherence of the systems involved?

6.6 Intimacy as Coherence Negotiation

Seen in this light, intimacy is not merely a source of gratification, attachment, or emotional support. It is a primary arena in which psychological systems negotiate shared coherence — in which the boundaries of self and other become permeable, regulatory resources are shared, and the stakes of integration are highest.

Intimacy is where the individual coherence structures developed in Sections 2–4 meet the distributed coherence dynamics developed in Sections 9–9. It is the smallest unit of shared coherence — the dyad — and its successes and failures reverberate across identity, mental health, moral life, and the broader social systems in which relationships are embedded.

The capacity for intimate coherence — for opening the self-model to another without collapse, for distributing regulatory load without dependency, for integrating sexual, emotional, and identity-level experience into a shared narrative — is among the most demanding coherence achievements available to human psychology. Its difficulty explains why relational distress is among the most common presenting complaints in clinical practice, and why its resolution often requires therapeutic work at every level: embodied, emotional, cognitive, identity, and meaning.

This section has extended the coherence framework to interpersonal domains: sexuality as embodied coherence exchange, attachment as co-regulation of coherence dynamics, and intimacy as the mutual permeability of self-models. These interpersonal processes are not additions to individual coherence but constitutive of it — the individual's coherence capacity is developed and maintained through relational coherence fields.

Section 7: Trauma, Neurodiversity, and Psychopathology — Coherence Collapse and Divergence

Psychology and psychiatry have long grouped trauma, neurodivergent conditions, and psychopathology under a single umbrella of "abnormality" — treating all three as departures from healthy functioning that require correction. From the perspective of Coherence Universalism, this grouping obscures a distinction that is both scientifically fundamental and ethically consequential.

Some conditions reflect **coherence collapse** — failures of integration that undermine viability and produce suffering. Others reflect **coherence divergence** — alternative but viable coherence strategies that differ from dominant norms without entailing dysfunction. Conflating the two leads to two symmetrical errors: treating genuine suffering as mere difference (and withholding needed care), or treating genuine difference as disorder (and imposing unnecessary correction). CU provides principled criteria for distinguishing them.

This section formalizes that distinction and develops its implications for trauma, neurodiversity, and psychopathology. With the elimination of the separate Trauma/Neurodiversity appendix from earlier drafts, this section serves as the primary treatment of these topics within the paper.

7.1 Two Principles: Collapse and Divergence

CU-Ψ7. Pathology as Non-Viable Coherence. A psychological system is pathological when it cannot maintain coherence across relevant domains and timescales sufficient to sustain agency, intelligibility, and integrated functioning — regardless of how common or uncommon its traits may be. This principle is the psychological instantiation of the foundational Coherence Collapse principle (CU-FP7), which holds that coherence can undergo catastrophic rather than merely gradual failure when regulatory capacity is exceeded.

CU-Ψ8. Divergence as Alternative Coherence. A psychological system is divergent but non-pathological when it maintains viable coherence through strategies that differ from dominant norms — when the system's integration is intact but organized along different dimensions, with different sensitivities, and under different regulatory priorities than the statistical majority.

The distinction is not between normal and abnormal but between viable and non-viable. A system that deviates radically from population norms but maintains integrated, self-regulating functioning across time is divergent, not pathological. A system that conforms to population norms in every respect but cannot sustain integration — that fragments under ordinary stress, that cannot maintain identity across competing demands, that loses agency through escalating self-deception — is pathological, however common its surface presentation may be.

This reframing has immediate diagnostic consequences. The guiding question shifts from "Does this system deviate from normal?" to "Can this system maintain viable coherence under its current conditions?" The answer depends not only on the system's internal organization but on the interaction between the system and its environment — a point that will prove critical for understanding neurodiversity.

7.2 Trauma as Coherence Catastrophe

Trauma is the most acute form of coherence collapse. The Consciousness paper (Section 11.5) developed the formal analysis: trauma is a sudden, large-magnitude increase in distortion D(u), in which the system's configuration is forced far from its coherence optimum. The traumatic event drives the system toward the boundary of its viability region V — and in severe cases, across local viability boundaries, forcing reorganization around a new, less optimal coherence configuration.

In terms of the Universal Flow Equation (CU-D1), the system's update dynamics are overwhelmed: the perturbation exceeds the system's capacity for coherence-preserving update. Coherence drive (CU-D2) remains operative — the system still presses toward whatever coherence it can maintain — but it now operates within a damaged landscape, navigating toward a lower coherence maximum than the one it inhabited before the traumatic event.

This formal picture makes precise what clinicians have long observed. Van der Kolk (2014) describes trauma as experience that overwhelms the organism's capacity to integrate — producing a state in which the body "keeps the score" even when conscious narrative processing has moved on. Herman (1992) characterizes traumatic events as those that overwhelm the ordinary human adaptations to life, producing a sense of helplessness and disconnection. Janoff-Bulman (1992) describes trauma as the shattering of fundamental assumptions about the world's benevolence, the world's meaningfulness, and the self's worthiness — assumptions that constitute, in CU terms, the core structure of the meaning map (CU-Ψ2).

CU unifies these clinical descriptions under a single structural account. Trauma is not defined by the objective severity of the event but by its effect on integration — by the magnitude of distortion D(u) it produces relative to the system's regulatory capacity. Two individuals may undergo similar events with radically different outcomes depending on developmental context, available social support, prior coherence capacity, and the relationship between the event and the system's identity-defining constraints (CU-I1). What renders an experience traumatic is the inability to incorporate it into an existing coherence structure without crossing viability boundaries.

7.2.1 The Characteristic Features of Trauma

The symptoms of post-traumatic stress follow directly from the formal analysis, each corresponding to a specific dimension of coherence failure:

Intrusive memories reflect failures of temporal coherence. The traumatic experience has not been incorporated into the system's narrative structure — it remains unintegrated, occupying a region of state space H that cannot be connected to the system's current coherence configuration without destabilizing identity (as analyzed in Section 2.4). The memory erupts into present awareness because it has not been temporally bound — it retains the phenomenological quality of present occurrence rather than past event.

Hyperarousal reflects persistent threat-prioritized regulation. The traumatic event has recalibrated the system's threat-detection sensitivity, permanently elevating the norepinephrine-mediated alarm response (Appendix C, §C.4). In formal terms, the system's coherence drive (CU-Ψ5) now operates with a threat bias: every perturbation is evaluated against the possibility of catastrophic coherence collapse, even when present conditions do not warrant it. The system cannot distinguish between signals that resemble the original threat and signals of genuine present danger — a generalization failure that reflects the depth of the constraint-reshaping produced by trauma.

Dissociation reflects fragmentation as a protective response. When the full impact of traumatic experience would overwhelm coherence entirely, the system partitions — isolating the traumatic material from the rest of experience. In the formal apparatus, dissociation corresponds to a partition of the state space: the system's configuration fragments into semi-independent subsystems, each maintaining local coherence within its partition but with reduced integration across partitions. Global C(u) decreases (because cross-partition integration is lost) while local coherence within each partition may be preserved or even enhanced. This is the formal expression of a clinical observation that dissociative parts can be internally coherent while being mutually inaccessible.

Emotional numbing reflects shutdown of regulatory signaling. The system suppresses the valence signals (CU-C3) that would guide reintegration because those signals, in the traumatic context, are overwhelming. Numbing is a local coherence strategy: it reduces the felt intensity of the coherence crisis, allowing moment-to-moment functioning. But it also disables the regulatory guidance that would support reintegration — trapping the system in a state of low felt distress and low integrative capacity.

These are not independent symptoms that happen to co-occur. They are coordinated expressions of a single structural condition: coherence collapse that the system has stabilized through emergency reorganization. Each symptom reflects a specific dimension of the system's attempt to maintain local coherence in the aftermath of global disruption.

7.2.2 Trauma, Identity, and Irreversibility

The Consciousness paper established that trauma reshapes the identity-defining constraints but does not replace them (CU-I3, Irreversible Path-Dependence). The traumatized system is the same system, now operating under altered constraints. The damage variable accumulates irreversibly: experience cannot be unlived; constraint-reshaping cannot be fully undone.

This has two consequences of profound psychological importance.

First, healing does not mean returning to the pre-traumatic state. That state is no longer accessible — the landscape has been permanently altered. Healing means finding a new coherence maximum that integrates the traumatic material — reducing D(u) not by returning to the original configuration but by discovering a configuration that accommodates the system's altered constraints. In clinical practice, this is what effective trauma therapy achieves: not the erasure of traumatic experience but its integration into a self-model and narrative that can sustain agency and meaning.

Second, post-traumatic growth becomes structurally intelligible. Some trauma survivors report that the reorganization forced by catastrophe led to configurations that are, in certain respects, more integrated than their pre-traumatic states — deeper values, clearer priorities, greater compassion, enhanced capacity for meaning. CU understands this as the system discovering a coherence maximum higher than any previously accessible — a configuration that could not have been reached without the perturbation of trauma but represents genuinely greater integration. The irreversibility that makes trauma damaging is the same irreversibility that makes growth possible: because the system cannot return to its prior state, it is forced to explore regions of the coherence landscape that were previously invisible.

7.2.3 Complex and Developmental Trauma

The formal analysis applies with particular force to complex trauma — prolonged, repeated exposure to coherence-overwhelming events, often in childhood and often within attachment relationships. Complex trauma, as described by Herman (1992) and van der Kolk (2014), produces damage that is more pervasive than single-event trauma because it disrupts coherence at the developmental level — reshaping the system's regulatory architecture during the period when that architecture is being constructed.

In CU terms, complex trauma does not merely displace the system from its coherence optimum; it deforms the coherence landscape itself. The system does not develop a healthy baseline from which it is subsequently displaced. It develops within a damaged landscape, building its regulatory capacities, self-model, and attachment strategies around the conditions of ongoing threat. The result is not a single D(u) spike but a chronically elevated baseline of distortion — a system that has never known undisturbed coherence and whose compensatory strategies are therefore woven into the fabric of identity rather than overlaid upon it.

This explains why complex trauma is so resistant to intervention and why its effects are so pervasive. The standard trauma model — perturbation followed by recovery toward baseline — does not apply when there is no unperturbed baseline to recover toward. Treatment must construct integrative capacity that was never developed, not merely restore capacity that was temporarily disrupted. This is a fundamentally different therapeutic challenge, and it is why trauma-informed approaches increasingly emphasize safety, relational repair, and long-term capacity-building over technique-focused processing of specific events.

7.2.4 Trauma as Loss of a Coherence Regime

The preceding analysis describes what trauma does to the system's configuration — how it displaces, fragments, and reorganizes. But the new material from the identity analysis (Section 5.1.1) permits a deeper characterization: trauma is not merely damage to a system; it is a topology change in the space of viable coherence strategies. The person does not merely lose stability; she loses the ability to stabilize using the same organizing principles she used before.

A mind maintains its psychological coherence by occupying a coherence regime — a set of beliefs, expectations, and predictive assumptions that jointly allow low prediction error across life situations. Consider a person whose implicit model includes: "people basically will not violate my bodily boundaries." This is not merely a belief; it is a load-bearing compression rule that keeps the model simple and reduces uncertainty across social interaction. When this assumption is shattered by sexual assault, the system cannot update locally. The violation produces prediction error so large that no incremental belief revision can absorb it without destroying the global consistency of the model.

The system therefore faces a forced choice: preserve the model (through denial, dissociation, or freezing) or update the model (which collapses large portions of the world-structure that depended on the violated assumption). This is why trauma feels world-destroying — not metaphorically but computationally. The event has invalidated a regime, not merely a belief.

After the regime collapses, the system still must maintain stability. But the previous high-level organizing assumptions are no longer admissible. So the mind retreats to lower-resolution coherence rules — "avoid situations," "avoid feeling," "control everything" — that require fewer assumptions about the world and therefore fewer opportunities for catastrophic prediction failure. These are not malfunctions. They are emergency stabilization at a lower-order attractor.

7.2.5 Failed Recovery as Downward Coherence Spiral

When initial coping strategies fail to restore a viable coherence regime, the system enters a progressive degradation cycle. Each compensatory mechanism further constrains the system's model class, narrowing the range of experiences it can tolerate and the range of interpretations it can sustain.

Avoidance reduces experiential data, which makes the model less accurate, which produces more prediction error, which motivates further retreat. Emotional numbing disables the regulatory signals that would guide reintegration, trapping the system in a low-information state that prevents learning. Substance use provides immediate coherence relief at the cost of long-term regulatory degradation. Each step is locally rational — each reduces the immediate coherence burden — but globally catastrophic, because each step further restricts the system's viable state space.

The trajectory is therefore a sequence of regime descents:

The system moves from a nuanced, flexible coherence regime to progressively simpler, more rigid, and more restricted ones — each capable of less integration, less ambiguity tolerance, and less adaptive response. At the terminal stage, the only stable regime is moment-to-moment survival regulation: the person's entire psychological architecture has been organized around threat management, with no remaining capacity for exploration, relationship, or meaning.

This is the structural description of what clinicians observe as chronic PTSD, severe dissociation, and the progressive narrowing of life that accompanies unresolved trauma. It is not a failure of will or a lack of effort. It is coherence optimization under progressively tighter constraints — the system doing the best it can within a state space that has been shrinking at every step.

7.2.6 Recovery as Phase Transition

If trauma is the loss of a coherence regime and failed recovery is progressive descent through lower-order regimes, then genuine recovery requires something more than incremental improvement. The person cannot simply return to the pre-traumatic regime because the organizing assumption that supported it has been logically falsified. The old belief — "the world is safe in the way I assumed" — is no longer tenable. No amount of therapy can make it true again, because the information cannot be unlearned.

Recovery therefore requires constructing a new, strictly more expressive coherence model — one capable of holding both realities simultaneously: safety exists *and* violation exists. The old regime could not represent that conjunction without contradiction. The new regime must.

This is a phase transition, not a gradual improvement. The system must cross an instability barrier — a region of the coherence landscape where no current regime stabilizes the system — before arriving at a higher-order configuration on the other side. During this crossing, coherence temporarily decreases. The system experiences increased distress, confusion, identity uncertainty, and vulnerability. This is the *constructive incoherence window*: a period in which the brain suspends its normal optimization long enough to rebuild its model class.

The phase-leap character of recovery explains several clinical observations. It explains why healing often feels worse before it feels better (Section 8.6). It explains why recovery is characteristically nonlinear — not a gradual upward slope but a discontinuous reorganization. It explains why the person who emerges from genuine trauma recovery is often not restored to her previous state but reorganized at a higher level of integration — with deeper values, clearer priorities, greater compassion, and enhanced capacity for meaning. This is post-traumatic growth in its structural form: the system has been forced to explore regions of the coherence landscape that were previously inaccessible, and has discovered a configuration more integrated than the one it lost.

The critical implication is that recovery cannot be achieved by argument, instruction, or insight alone. The system cannot *think* its way across the instability barrier. It must *survive* crossing it — which requires the conditions described in Section 7.

7.2.7 Self-Deception in the Aftermath of Trauma

Section 5.5 defined self-deception as meaning-map distortion that preserves local coherence at the expense of global integrability. In the aftermath of trauma, self-deception takes on a specific and clinically consequential form: it becomes the mechanism by which the system prevents the collapse of its remaining coherence regime when truth would force a regime transition it cannot yet survive.

After traumatic violation, the system faces two incompatible constraints: represent reality accurately, and maintain a stable self-model. But the trauma implies that accurate representation destabilizes the self-model — that seeing clearly would overwhelm the system's current integrative capacity. The system therefore solves an optimization problem: minimize the combined cost of prediction error and identity destabilization. When truth is too expensive, the system selectively distorts reality.

The resulting distortions are not random. They minimize destabilization cost with remarkable precision: "I deserved it" preserves the model of a just world (reducing the scope of the revision needed). "I misunderstood" preserves the trustworthiness of the violator (reducing relational disruption). "I'm overreacting" preserves the assumption that the world is safe (reducing the scope of threat recalibration). "I chose it" preserves the model of personal agency (preventing the devastating recognition of powerlessness). Each of these distortions is locally coherent and globally costly — and each is precisely targeted at the load-bearing assumption that the trauma most directly threatened.

This reframing has immediate clinical implications. Confronting self-deception directly — pushing truth before the system can survive it — typically increases rigidity rather than producing insight. The nervous system responds to premature destabilization by strengthening its defenses: denial deepens, rationalization becomes more elaborate, emotional numbing intensifies. The system is preventing uncontrolled regime transition — and it is right to do so, because uncontrolled transition produces not healing but retraumatization.

The therapeutic implication follows: therapy should not attack defenses. It should make them unnecessary. When external coherence support is sufficient — when safety, trust, and relational regulation are established — the cost function changes. Identity destabilization decreases because the system is no longer maintaining coherence alone. Truth becomes cheaper than distortion. At that point, the person spontaneously revises beliefs — not through persuasion or confrontation but through release. The defenses dissolve because they are no longer needed.

For survivors, this reframing offers something important: *you did not refuse the truth. Your nervous system protected you until truth became survivable.* Self-deception after trauma is not a moral failure; it is a temporary scaffold for identity reconstruction.

7.2.8 Memory Reconsolidation and the Mechanism of Phase-Leap Recovery

The phase-leap model of recovery (Section 7.2.6) describes the structural requirement — the system must cross an instability barrier to reach a higher-order regime. Memory reconsolidation provides the biological mechanism by which this crossing occurs.

Modern reconsolidation research (Nader, Schafe, & Le Doux, 2000; Lane et al., 2015) has established that when a consolidated memory is reactivated, it enters a labile state in which it can be modified before being re-stabilized. The reconsolidation window is brief — typically minutes to hours — and during this window the memory is genuinely editable: its emotional valence, associative connections, and interpretive framing can be altered.

In CU terms, a traumatic memory is not merely an event record. It is a constraint bundle — a set of high-precision priors that shape threat prediction, identity assumptions, and the range of coherence regimes the system treats as admissible. The memory stabilizes the current (lower-order) regime by continuously enforcing the constraints that the trauma produced. Healing requires rewriting these constraints, and reconsolidation provides the biological window in which rewriting is possible.

The successful therapeutic sequence corresponds precisely to the reconsolidation protocol: (i) reactivate the memory enough to open the lability window — the constraint bundle becomes temporarily editable; (ii) introduce a disconfirming experience while the window is open — not argument or interpretation, but lived experience that violates the trauma-constraint (the presence of safety where the constraint predicts danger, the experience of trust where the constraint predicts violation); (iii) allow the system to re-encode the memory in a form compatible with a higher-order regime — the constraint bundle is rewritten, and the regime transition becomes possible.

This is the biological instantiation of the constructive incoherence window. The system temporarily tolerates incoherence while the constraint bundle is being rewritten. If the process succeeds, the higher-order regime stabilizes. If the process is interrupted — by premature closure, overwhelming affect, or insufficient safety — the constraint bundle reconsolidates in its original form, and the barrier may become harder to cross on subsequent attempts.

The reconsolidation framework also explains why insight alone rarely heals trauma. Semantic updating — knowing intellectually that "it wasn't my fault" — does not rewrite the constraint bundle, because the constraint bundle operates at the level of implicit prediction, not explicit belief. The constraint must be violated experientially, not merely contradicted propositionally. This is the structural reason that healing requires relationship, embodiment, and lived safety — not merely understanding.

7.2.9 The Social Transmission of Trauma

The preceding analysis focused on trauma within the individual. But CU's framework reveals a mechanism by which unresolved individual trauma propagates through social systems, creating cascading coherence degradation at collective scales. This mechanism — developed more fully in the forthcoming Social Dynamics paper — has its roots in the psychology of self-deception described in Section 7.2.7.

The sequence operates as follows. When a person stabilizes at a low-order coherence regime sustained by self-deception, the resulting configuration has characteristic properties: rigidity (high-precision priors, low revisability), narrow time horizon (short-term threat management dominates), and externalization (stability maintained by exporting incoherence to others). The person whose internal coherence depends on controlling others, scapegoating, or moral absolutism is not pursuing harm for its own sake; she is maintaining the only stable regime available to her. But the maintenance of that regime systematically generates coherence threats for others — through domination, betrayal, deception, or coercive control — which produces new trauma in those others, who then face their own regime collapses and may stabilize through their own self-deceptive strategies.

This yields a general principle: self-deception is the mechanism by which unresolved trauma becomes socially transmissible. The trauma does not propagate through explicit memory or narrative transmission. It propagates through the behavioral consequences of rigidified coherence

— through the harm that rigid, self-deceiving systems inflict on others in the course of maintaining their own stability.

The sequence — trauma → self-deception → rigidity → externalization → harm → new trauma — constitutes a positive feedback loop in social instability. Unaddressed, it produces the escalating cycles of violence, domination, and retribution that characterize much of human history. Addressing it requires not merely individual healing but the creation of conditions that interrupt the loop at multiple points: trauma-informed institutions that prevent the initial regime collapse from becoming permanent; accountability structures that constrain externalization without further traumatizing the person held accountable; and cultural frameworks that permit the revision of rigid beliefs without requiring identity destruction.

The ethical and political dimensions of this dynamic — including the claim that much of what humanity calls "evil" is coherent behavior within a collapsed regime — are developed in CU — Ethics. The institutional and collective dimensions — including how economic precarity mechanically compresses the coherence capacity of entire populations, amplifying the transmission cycle — are developed in the forthcoming Social Dynamics paper. The psychology paper's contribution is to establish the individual mechanism: how trauma produces self-deception, how self-deception produces harm, and how harm regenerates trauma in others.

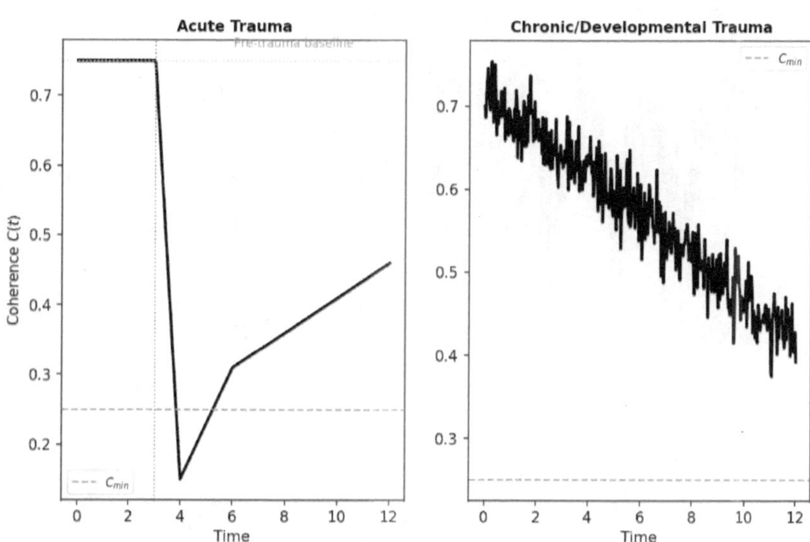

Figure 7. *Trauma as coherence catastrophe. Left: Acute trauma produces sudden coherence collapse below C_min, followed by partial recovery that may not reach pre--trauma levels. Right: Chronic or developmental trauma produces gradual coherence erosion with increasing noise, eventually approaching the collapse threshold. The two trajectories produce distinct clinical presentations but share a common structure: loss of integrated self-regulation across time.*

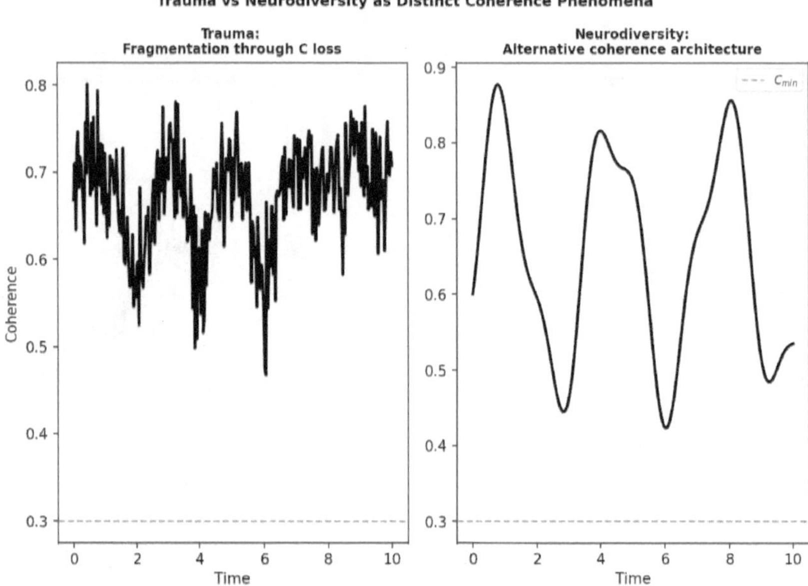

Figure 8. Trauma and neurodiversity as distinct coherence phenomena. Trauma (left) produces fragmentation through catastrophic coherence loss; neurodiversity (right) represents alternative coherence architectures that achieve integration through non--standard pathways.

7.3 Neurodiversity as Coherence Divergence

Neurodivergent conditions — including autism, ADHD, dyslexia, and related cognitive profiles — are frequently classified as disorders because they diverge from statistically dominant patterns of cognitive and social organization. From the perspective of CU-Ψ8 (Divergence as Alternative Coherence), many such conditions are better understood as alternative coherence strategies — systems that integrate experience along different dimensions, with different regulatory priorities, and under different sensitivities than the neurotypical majority.

7.3.1 Different Strategies, Not Failed Strategies

Neurodivergent systems often exhibit: different salience weighting in meaning space M — attending intensely to patterns, details, or regularities that neurotypical systems filter out; heightened coherence drive (CU-Ψ5) in specific domains, producing deep expertise, pattern recognition, or systematic thinking at the cost of flexibility in other domains; reduced tolerance for certain forms of incoherence that neurotypical systems accept without distress, including social ambiguity, sensory unpredictability, and arbitrary convention; and reliance on non--social or non-narrative regulatory pathways — maintaining coherence through systemization, routine, sensory management, or logical analysis rather than through the social attunement and narrative integration that dominate neurotypical regulation.

These are not deficits. They are different configurations in the coherence landscape — alternative navigational strategies that prioritize different dimensions of integration. An autistic system that achieves profound coherence in its domain of intense interest while struggling with social small talk has not failed at coherence; it has achieved coherence along different dimensions than its social environment demands.

7.3.2 Pathology at the Interface

Difficulties arise primarily at the interface between the neurodivergent system and its environment. When environments are optimized for neurotypical coherence strategies — when social contexts demand rapid processing of implicit cues, sensory environments impose unpredictable stimulation, and institutional structures require regulatory strategies that the system does not possess — the neurodivergent system experiences elevated IES (CU-Ψ4) despite intact or superior integrative capacity in other domains.

This interface-level analysis explains several patterns that the deficit model cannot:

It explains why the same individual can appear profoundly disabled in one context and exceptionally capable in another. The system's coherence capacity is not globally impaired; it is differently organized. Contexts that align with the system's strategy reveal its capacity; contexts that conflict with the strategy reveal its vulnerability.

It explains why forced normalization often increases distress rather than reducing it. Interventions that suppress the system's native coherence strategy — that demand neurotypical social performance, suppress stimming or other regulatory behaviors, or impose arbitrary routines — raise regulatory load without providing compensatory support. In CU terms, they increase IES by removing the system's primary coherence-maintenance tools while imposing coherence demands the system cannot meet with alternative tools. The result is not improved functioning but elevated distress, exhaustion, and eventual breakdown — the pattern clinically recognized as autistic burnout.

It explains why accommodation is often more effective than remediation. Modifying the environment to align with the system's coherence strategy — reducing sensory overload, providing clear expectations, allowing alternative regulatory behaviors, structuring social interaction to reduce ambiguity — lowers IES without requiring the system to abandon viable strategies. The system's coherence improves not because it has been fixed but because its environment has been adjusted to match its actual organization.

7.3.3 When Divergence Becomes Distress

The distinction between divergence and pathology is not absolute. Neurodivergent systems can and do experience genuine coherence collapse — not because of their divergent organization per se, but because sustained interface mismatch produces chronic IES that eventually overwhelms regulatory capacity. The result is comorbid anxiety, depression, trauma responses, and identity fragmentation — genuine pathology that emerges not from the neurodivergent architecture but from the cumulative cost of operating under conditions that do not support it.

This distinction matters clinically. Treating the comorbid pathology without addressing the interface mismatch that produced it is treating symptoms while maintaining the cause. Effective intervention for neurodivergent individuals in distress typically requires both: coherence restoration (addressing the accumulated damage) and environmental alignment (reducing the ongoing source of excessive regulatory load).

7.4 Psychopathology as Persistent Coherence Failure

With CU-Ψ7 and CU-Ψ8 established, we can characterize psychopathology in general: it is persistent failure to maintain viable coherence across relevant domains and timescales. This definition is structural, not statistical. It does not depend on deviation from population norms but on whether the system can sustain agency, intelligibility, and integrated functioning. Psychopathology instantiates the dynamics principle CU-D9 (Multi-Scale Failure): when coherence degrades at one scale —

perceptual, emotional, cognitive, identity, or social — the failure propagates across scales, producing the characteristic comorbidity and symptom migration that diagnostic categories struggle to explain.

7.4.1 Why Symptoms Cluster and Shift

A longstanding puzzle in psychopathology is comorbidity: why do diagnostic categories overlap so extensively? Why do anxiety and depression co-occur far more often than chance would predict? Why does trauma increase risk for virtually every subsequent disorder? Why do symptoms often shift over the course of an illness — presenting as anxiety at one point, depression at another, substance use at a third?

CU provides a structural answer. When coherence is compromised at a deep level — at the level of identity, meaning, or regulatory architecture — the resulting dysfunction is not confined to a single domain. It manifests across domains, and the specific surface expression depends on context, resources, and the compensatory strategies the system can access. Diagnostic categories capture surface patterns; coherence failure captures the underlying structural condition that generates those patterns.

In formal terms, a deep distortion D(u) produces a family of surface configurations rather than a single stable state. The system, pressed against the boundary of V, shifts between compensatory strategies — each producing a different symptom profile while the underlying coherence failure persists. Anxiety, depression, substance use, compulsive behavior, and relational dysfunction are not separate disorders that happen to co-occur; they are different faces of the same structural condition, viewed from different angles at different times.

This also explains why narrow interventions often produce symptom substitution rather than genuine recovery. Addressing the anxiety without addressing the underlying coherence failure may produce improvement in anxiety measures while the underlying distortion D(u) expresses itself through a different channel — as depression, as somatic complaints, as relational withdrawal. The distortion migrates because the structural condition has not been resolved.

7.4.2 Specific Pathologies as Coherence Configurations

Several major categories of psychopathology can be precisely located within the coherence landscape:

Anxiety disorders (previewed in Section 4.5) reflect hyper-activation of coherence drive without effective resolution — the system chronically detects incoherence it cannot repair. Generalized anxiety reflects multi--dimensional sensitivity across meaning space M. Panic disorder reflects catastrophic interpretation of incoherence signals — the system misreads ordinary perturbation as viability threat, producing a self-amplifying cycle. Obsessive-compulsive patterns reflect rigid local coherence strategies: the ritual reduces local IES temporarily while preventing the flexible integration that would resolve the underlying conflict. The compulsion persists because it works locally even as it fails globally — the signature of CU-Ψ6.

Depressive disorders (also previewed in Section 4.5) reflect motivational collapse in a local minimum — the system registers incoherence but perceives no navigable gradient. The formal analysis is precise: the system occupies a configuration in H that is locally stable (no nearby state is better) but globally suboptimal (much higher coherence is possible but inaccessible from the current position). The system is not indifferent; it is trapped. Coherence drive remains active — which is why depression involves suffering rather than emptiness — but the gradient is flat or descending in every accessible direction.

Personality disorders reflect deep attractor structures (Appendix F) that are globally maladaptive but locally self-reinforcing. Borderline personality organization, for instance, involves chronic instability of the self-model, oscillation between idealization and devaluation of others, and difficulty maintaining coherence across relational contexts. In CU terms, the system lacks a stable basin of attraction for identity — the coherence landscape around the self has no dominant minimum, producing the characteristic pattern of intense but unstable relationships, impulsive behavior, and identity disturbance that the clinical literature describes. Narcissistic personality organization involves a different configuration: a self-model maintained through systematic meaning-map distortion (CU-Ψ11), in which the system's FCS depends on continuous external validation and the suppression of any information that would threaten the inflated self-assessment. The strategy maintains identity coherence at the cost of escalating self-deception and progressive disconnection from reality.

Psychotic disorders involve the most severe forms of coherence failure: breakdown of the reality-testing functions that anchor meaning maps to the external world (CU-C6, World-Constrained Coherence). Delusions represent coherence constructions that have become decoupled from environmental constraint — internally consistent narratives that preserve meaning and agency but are no longer correctable by sensory evidence. Hallucinations reflect failures of the integration processes that normally distinguish internally generated from externally sourced signals. The system maintains coherence — delusions are often remarkably well-organized — but it maintains coherence of the wrong kind: internal consistency without external constraint, map without territory.

7.4.3 The Continuum of Coherence Compromise

CU implies that psychopathology is not categorical but dimensional. Between full coherence and total collapse lies a continuum of increasingly compromised integration. Every person experiences transient incoherence — moments of confusion, ambivalence, self-contradiction, or regulatory failure. What distinguishes psychopathology from ordinary difficulty is persistence, pervasiveness, and the system's inability to restore integration without intervention.

This dimensional view is consistent with the increasing empirical evidence that diagnostic boundaries are more fluid than categorical systems suggest. The Research Domain Criteria (RDoC) framework developed by the National Institute of Mental Health reflects a similar intuition: that psychopathology is better understood through dimensional constructs (negative valence systems, positive valence systems, cognitive systems, social processes, arousal/regulatory systems) than through discrete categories. CU provides the structural rationale for this dimensional approach: these constructs correspond to dimensions of the coherence landscape, and their disruption reflects the multi-dimensional character of coherence failure.

7.5 Reframing Diagnosis and Understanding

The coherence framework reframes both diagnosis and clinical understanding.

Diagnosis shifts from pattern-matching symptoms to a checklist toward identifying where and how coherence has failed. The guiding questions become: Which dimensions of the coherence landscape are compromised? Is the failure acute (trauma) or chronic (developmental, structural)? Is the primary problem displacement from a coherence optimum (the system's architecture is intact but its configuration has been disrupted) or decline of the coherence optimum itself (the system's regulatory capacity has been degraded)? Is the distress a consequence of genuine coherence failure or of interface mismatch between a divergent but viable system and an inhospitable environment?

Understanding shifts from deficit-based to structural. The person presenting with anxiety, depression, or relational difficulty is not broken. She is a coherence-maintaining system that has encountered conditions exceeding her regulatory capacity — or that has adopted compensatory strategies whose local success is producing global costs. The symptoms are not random or meaningless; they are the system's best available response to its coherence situation. Understanding them requires understanding the landscape, not merely cataloging the surface features.

Recovery is reframed as the restoration of integrative capacity — not the elimination of all distress or the achievement of some idealized state of well-being but the recovery of the system's ability to experience, respond, and act without fragmentation. A person who has recovered from trauma may still carry the marks of her experience — the constraints have been irreversibly reshaped (CU-I3) — but she can integrate that experience into a coherent trajectory rather than being organized around it. Recovery is the difference between a life shaped by trauma and a life shattered by it.

This section has reframed psychopathology as coherence failure — not disease entities but patterns of integration breakdown. Trauma constricts the viability space within which the system can maintain coherence. Neurodivergent conditions represent alternative coherence strategies that may succeed in some environments while struggling in others. Recovery is the restoration of integrative capacity, not the elimination of all distress.

Section 8: Therapy, Healing Practices, and Psychoactive Substances — Coherence Modulation

Psychological interventions differ widely in technique, theory, and cultural framing. Cognitive therapies target beliefs and thought patterns. Psychodynamic approaches explore unconscious conflict and narrative integration. Somatic therapies address bodily regulation. Pharmacological interventions alter neurochemical signaling. Psychedelic-assisted approaches temporarily dissolve constraint structures to enable reorganization. Rituals, music, movement, and contemplative practices operate outside conventional clinical categories entirely. Each tradition has its own explanatory vocabulary, its own account of what has gone wrong, and its own theory of what healing requires.

From the perspective of Coherence Universalism, these differences obscure a deeper commonality. Every effective psychological intervention works by modulating coherence — by restoring integration, reducing regulatory load, or enabling reorganization at a higher level. This commonality is not a vague gesture toward "everything is connected." It is a precise structural claim with testable implications.

CU-Ψ9. Therapy as Coherence Modulation. Therapeutic intervention restores psychological viability by modulating the system's position within its coherence landscape — reducing distortion D(u), lowering Inverse Entropic Stress (IES, CU-Ψ4), increasing the Field Coherence Score (FCS, CU-Ψ3), or enabling transition to a more globally coherent attractor basin.

Therapy, in this sense, is not the correction of error, the imposition of normality, or the elimination of distress. It is the guided restoration of a system's capacity to maintain coherence across domains and timescales — an instance of the dynamics principle CU-D8 (Repair), which holds that coherence restoration, not mere symptom suppression, is the mechanism underlying genuine recovery.

8.1 The Common Factors Problem

One of the most robust and most embarrassing findings in psychotherapy research is the "Dodo bird verdict" (Rosenzweig, 1936;

Luborsky, Singer, & Luborsky, 1975): different therapeutic modalities produce broadly comparable outcomes despite radically different theoretical frameworks. Cognitive-behavioral therapy, psychodynamic therapy, humanistic therapy, and interpersonal therapy all yield similar effect sizes for depression, anxiety, and general psychological distress. Wampold's (2001, 2015) meta-analytic work demonstrates that common factors — the therapeutic alliance, therapist empathy, patient expectation, and the provision of a coherent rationale for suffering — account for far more outcome variance than specific techniques.

This finding has been a persistent theoretical puzzle. If therapies with contradictory theories of mind produce equivalent results, what is actually doing the work?

CU provides a structural answer: the common factors are coherence factors. The therapeutic alliance provides interpersonal co-regulation (the adult analogue of the attachment-based distributed coherence described in Section 6.1), reducing the system's regulatory isolation and extending its effective viability region V. Therapist empathy provides the experience of being understood — of having one's internal configuration accurately mirrored by another system — which reduces the sense that one's coherence crisis is unique, incomprehensible, or shameful. Patient expectation restores gradient visibility: the belief that improvement is possible re-establishes a navigable coherence gradient where previously the landscape appeared flat. And the provision of a coherent rationale — regardless of its specific content — provides a meaning-map framework within which suffering becomes intelligible rather than chaotic, which directly reduces IES by converting unstructured distress into structured challenge.

The common factors work because they address the structural preconditions for coherence repair. Specific techniques then operate within this prepared context, targeting particular dimensions of coherence failure. Both are necessary; neither is sufficient alone. This explains why technique without alliance fails (the system cannot reorganize without relational safety) and why alliance without technique plateaus (the system feels supported but has no direction for reorganization).

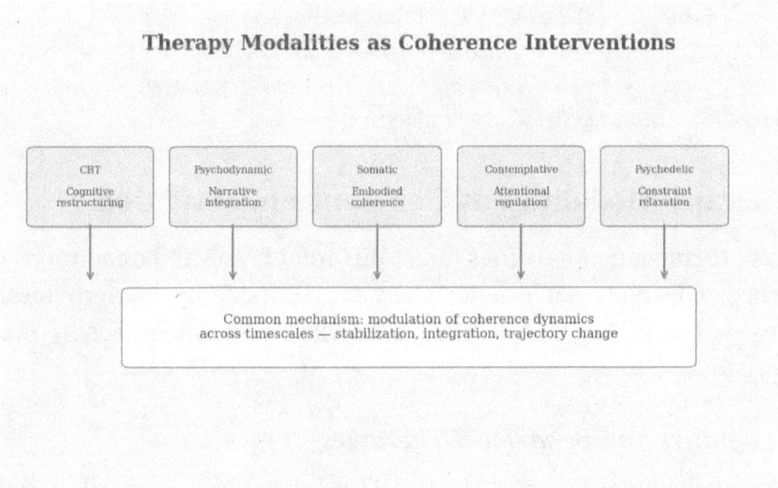

Figure 9. *Therapy as coherence modulation. The therapeutic trajectory (solid) shows non-monotonic progress: temporary dips in coherence are expected as the system reorganizes around new integrative structures. The dotted line shows the no-intervention baseline. The framework predicts that effective therapy produces a characteristic signature: initial destabilization followed by re-stabilization at a higher coherence level, with setbacks as part of the process rather than evidence of failure.*

Therapy Modalities Mapped to Coherence Mechanisms

Therapy Modality

Coherence Mechanism Targeted

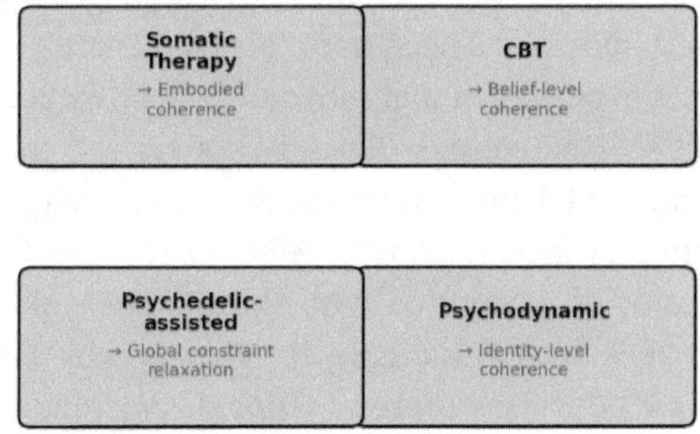

Figure 10. *Therapy modalities mapped to coherence mechanisms. CBT targets belief-level coherence; psychodynamic approaches address identity-level coherence; somatic therapies restore embodied coherence; psychedelic-assisted therapy operates via global constraint relaxation and reorganization.*

8.2 Therapy Modalities as Coherence Interventions

Different therapeutic modalities target different layers and dimensions of coherence. CU does not privilege any single modality but provides a framework for understanding what each does and when each is most appropriate.

8.2.1 Cognitive and Behavioral Therapies

Cognitive-behavioral therapy (Beck, 1976; Ellis, 1962) primarily targets representational coherence — the alignment between the system's beliefs, interpretations, and the evidence available. By identifying cognitive distortions, testing beliefs against evidence, and building alternative interpretations, CBT reduces conflicts between perception, expectation, and action.

In CU terms, CBT operates on the meaning map Φ directly. It identifies points where Φ has become distorted — where the map's representation of reality has diverged from the territory in ways that produce elevated IES — and systematically corrects the distortion. Behavioral activation adds a complementary mechanism: by re-engaging with activities that produce positive valence, the system discovers that the coherence landscape contains navigable gradients that depression had rendered invisible. The system does not merely learn that its beliefs were wrong; it experiences that movement is possible.

CBT's effectiveness depends not on the truth of any single revised belief but on whether the revised meaning map supports more integrated navigation of meaning space. A belief revision that is technically accurate but cannot be integrated with the system's identity and values will not reduce IES; it will increase it. This is why CBT sometimes fails: the technique addresses representational coherence without attending to the identity-level coherence constraints that make certain beliefs necessary for the system's current stability.

8.2.2 Psychodynamic and Narrative Therapies

Psychodynamic therapy (Freud, 1917; Mitchell & Black, 1995) and narrative therapy (White & Epston, 1990) target temporal and identity coherence. They aim to integrate past experiences, unresolved conflicts, and disowned affect into a narrative that the self-model can sustain.

In CU terms, psychodynamic therapy works by reducing the amount of experience that has been excluded from the meaning map. Repression, in this framework, is a form of meaning-map distortion (CU-Ψ11): material that cannot be integrated without threatening identity coherence is excluded from Φ, producing a map that is locally stable but globally impoverished. Therapy makes the excluded material accessible — not by forcing awareness but by creating conditions of sufficient safety (reduced IES) that the system can tolerate the temporary destabilization of incorporating what was excluded.

Insight is therapeutic not because it reveals hidden causes in a mechanical sense but because it enables previously fragmented material to be coherently incorporated into the temporal structure of the self. The "aha" moment in psychodynamic therapy is, in CU terms, the felt experience of a sudden reduction in D(u): material that was producing chronic distortion by its exclusion has been integrated, and the system's configuration moves closer to a coherence optimum.

Narrative therapy operates by a related mechanism at the level of story structure. By helping the person re-author the story she tells about her life — identifying neglected plotlines, surfacing alternative interpretations, and constructing narratives that emphasize agency and meaning rather than victimhood and inevitability — narrative therapy restructures the temporal dimension of the meaning map without requiring explicit engagement with unconscious conflict.

8.2.3 Somatic and Embodied Therapies

Somatic therapies (Levine, 1997; Ogden, Minton, & Pain, 2006) address physiological coherence — the bodily layer of integration that often operates beneath conscious awareness and below the reach of verbal intervention.

Trauma frequently disrupts bodily regulation before it disrupts explicit belief (Section 7.2). The body's emergency responses — fight, flight, freeze — may remain activated long after the threat has passed, maintaining a state of physiological incoherence that pervades all higher-level functioning. Somatic interventions that restore rhythm, breath, posture, and movement re-establish foundational coherence upon which higher-level integration depends.

In CU terms, somatic therapy operates at the base of the coherence hierarchy. The body is the system's primary interface with its own viability constraints — the level at which the Consciousness paper's forcing conditions (CF-1 through CF-5) are most directly realized. When bodily coherence is disrupted, the entire coherence architecture is destabilized, because the system's regulatory foundation has been compromised. Restoring physiological regulation does not resolve the meaning-level or identity-level dimensions of trauma, but it provides the regulatory floor from which higher-level integration becomes possible.

This is why somatic approaches are often essential for complex trauma (Section 7.2.3), where the disruption occurred during the period when the regulatory architecture was being constructed. Cognitive and narrative approaches require a system that can tolerate the affect mobilized by integration work. When the physiological foundation for affect tolerance is absent — when the body cannot regulate arousal well enough to support reflective processing — somatic work must precede or accompany higher-level intervention.

8.2.4 Relational and Systems Therapies

Relational therapies — including couples therapy, family systems approaches (Minuchin, 1974; Bowen, 1978), and group therapy — address interpersonal coherence directly. They recognize that the system requiring intervention is often not the individual but the relational field in which the individual is embedded.

In CU terms, relational therapies modulate shared coherence fields (CU-Ψ12). They work by restructuring the coordination dynamics (Rung 23) that maintain or undermine coherence across the dyad, family, or group. A couple locked in a pattern of anxious pursuit and avoidant withdrawal is not two individually pathological systems; it is a dyadic system whose shared coherence strategy has become self-reinforcing and globally maladaptive — each partner's regulatory behavior amplifying the other's distress in a feedback loop that neither can exit unilaterally.

Systems therapy intervenes at the level of the pattern rather than the individual, restructuring the relational dynamics so that the shared coherence field supports rather than undermines each system's individual integration.

8.2.5 The Unified Mechanism: Borrowed Coherence

The regime-change model of trauma (Section 7.2.6) established that genuine recovery requires crossing an instability barrier — a region of the coherence landscape where no current regime stabilizes the system. This crossing cannot be accomplished by the system alone, because the system's own regulatory capacity is precisely what has been compromised. The system cannot remain stable while updating.

All effective trauma therapies therefore share a structural requirement that goes deeper than the common factors identified in Section 8.1: they must provide *borrowed coherence* — an external source of regulatory stability that holds the system together while its internal model reorganizes. Without borrowed coherence, entering the constructive incoherence window (Section 7.2.6) produces not healing but retraumatization: the instability overwhelms the system, triggers emergency responses, and reinforces the barriers that prevent regime transition.

The different modalities described above can now be understood as providing borrowed coherence through different channels:

Exposure therapy borrows coherence from environmental structure. The repeated, controlled presentation of trauma-associated stimuli in a safe context provides the system with a reliable stream of disconfirming evidence: the stimulus occurs, and catastrophe does not follow. The environmental predictability lowers the energy cost of the regime transition, making the instability barrier crossable. Exposure does not "desensitize" — it makes the phase transition energetically affordable.

EMDR borrows coherence from cognitive load management. The bilateral stimulation occupies attentional resources that would otherwise be consumed by emergency regulation, creating a controlled bandwidth partition: the system can process the traumatic memory without being overwhelmed by it. Working memory is split between the external task (which provides stability) and the internal reprocessing (which enables constraint rewriting). The result is controlled destabilization with cognitive scaffolding.

Psychodynamic and narrative therapies borrow coherence from temporal structure. By providing a framework within which fragmented experience can be sequenced, contextualized, and given meaning, these approaches supply the integrative scaffolding that the system's own narrative capacity cannot currently provide.

Somatic therapies borrow coherence from the body's own regulatory architecture. By re-establishing physiological rhythm, breath regulation, and movement patterns, somatic work restores the foundational coherence layer upon which all higher integration depends — providing a floor of stability from which the system can tolerate the destabilization required for regime change.

Deep trust relationships. Whether therapeutic or personal — borrow coherence from another nervous system. This is the most fundamental channel. When a person's coherence is maintained partly through attunement with a trusted other, the dyadic system has greater regulatory capacity than either individual alone. The person can experience previously impossible states — grief, rage, terror, helplessness — without fragmentation, because the relational field provides the stability that her internal architecture cannot.

In every case, the principle is the same: the system enters the instability region not alone but supported, and the support makes the difference between productive reorganization and retraumatizing collapse. The memory reconsolidation framework (Section 7.2.8) specifies the biological mechanism — the lability window during which constraint bundles can be rewritten — but borrowed coherence specifies the *structural precondition* for that window to open safely.

This unification explains why therapy modalities with radically different theories of change produce comparable outcomes (Section 8.1): they all provide borrowed coherence, and borrowed coherence is the rate-limiting factor in regime transition. Specific techniques matter because they determine *which dimension* of coherence is supported. But no technique works without the relational and environmental safety that makes the instability barrier crossable.

8.3 Pharmacological Interventions

Pharmacological interventions modulate coherence at the neurochemical level — altering the regulatory parameters that govern how the system detects, pursues, and stabilizes coherence. Appendix C develops the neurotransmitter framework in detail; here we address the therapeutic logic.

When effective, pharmacological interventions lower the cost of maintaining coherence, allowing psychological reorganization that would otherwise be inaccessible. An SSRI that stabilizes serotonergic baseline regulation (Appendix C, §C.3) reduces the affective volatility that makes meaning-map navigation chaotic — not by resolving the underlying coherence challenge but by lowering the regulatory noise against which resolution must be attempted. A stimulant that sharpens attentional coherence (Appendix C, §C.2) may enable a neurodivergent system to function in environments optimized for neurotypical regulation — reducing interface-level IES (Section 7.3.2) without altering the system's underlying architecture.

When misapplied, pharmacological interventions suppress signals without resolving underlying incoherence (Section 4.4). An anxiolytic that dampens threat signaling provides immediate IES reduction but prevents the system from accessing the regulatory information it needs for reintegration — the mechanism of signal suppression without resolution developed in Appendix D, §D.4. Chronic use under these conditions produces dependence: the system becomes organized around the pharmacological suppression of coherence signals rather than around the resolution of the coherence challenges those signals track.

The fundamental question for any pharmacological intervention, from a CU perspective, is: does it reduce IES in a way that enables coherence repair, or does it reduce felt IES in a way that prevents it? The distinction is between lowering the actual regulatory load (making integration possible) and lowering the felt registration of regulatory load (making integration unnecessary-seeming but still undone).

Appendix D develops specific substance profiles — SSRIs, stimulants, anxiolytics, mood stabilizers, and widely used non--pharmaceutical substances — through this evaluative lens.

8.4 Psychedelic-Assisted Therapy

Psychedelics occupy a distinct category in the coherence framework. They do not merely alter regulatory parameters; they temporarily dissolve the constraint structures within which coherence is organized — producing a fundamentally different kind of therapeutic opportunity and a fundamentally different kind of risk.

The neuropharmacological mechanism — particularly for classic serotonergic psychedelics (psilocybin, LSD, DMT) — involves reduction of default mode network activity, increased global functional connectivity, and relaxation of the top-down predictive constraints that normally organize perception, cognition, and self-modeling (Carhart-Harris et al., 2014; Carhart-Harris & Friston, 2019). In CU terms, psychedelics temporarily reduce the depth and rigidity of the system's attractor basins, increasing the state space available for exploration and reducing the energy barrier between configurations that are normally separated.

This has several coherence implications. Material that has been excluded from the meaning map — through repression, dissociation, or self-deception — becomes accessible because the constraints that maintained its exclusion have been relaxed. Attractor structures that have become rigid (the compulsive, the addictive, the identity-protective) are temporarily loosened, allowing the system to explore alternative configurations. The self-model, normally maintained with considerable regulatory effort, may partially dissolve — producing experiences of ego dissolution, boundary-loss, or oceanic connection that the Consciousness paper (Section 11.3) analyzes as changes in the system's identity-maintenance dynamics.

The therapeutic potential lies not in the experience itself but in how coherence is re-established afterward. When psychedelic experience is followed by integration — supported by therapeutic context, relationship, and meaning-making — the system may reorganize around a new, more globally coherent configuration. The temporary dissolution of constraints allows the system to "reset" its attractor landscape, potentially escaping local minima that trapped it in depression, addiction, or rigid self-deception.

Without integration, the same dissolution that enables reorganization can produce destabilization. The system's constraint structures are relaxed but no alternative structure is offered. The result may be fragmentation, increased IES, identity confusion, or spiritual emergency — the system has been shaken loose from its attractor but has not landed in a new one. This is why set, setting, and post-experience integration are not optional additions to psychedelic therapy but structural necessities — they provide the coherence scaffolding within which reorganization can occur safely.

8.5 Non-Clinical Coherence Practices

Psychology's clinical focus can obscure the fact that most coherence modulation throughout human history has occurred outside therapeutic contexts. Music, dance, ritual, physical exercise, contemplative practice, communal worship, artistic expression, and narrative traditions all function as coherence modulators — technologies for synchronizing affect, embodiment, and attention, often within shared social contexts.

Their persistence across cultures and centuries reflects their effectiveness as coherence technologies. They work because they address the same structural needs that therapy addresses — regulation, integration, meaning, and connection — through means that are accessible, repeatable, and often communal.

Contemplative practices — meditation, prayer, yoga, centering practices — modulate coherence by training the system's capacity for regulatory stability and attentional integration. Mindfulness meditation, for instance, develops the system's ability to observe its own coherence dynamics without reactive engagement — to register perturbation without being destabilized by it. In CU terms, contemplative practice expands the system's effective viability region V by increasing its tolerance for states that would otherwise trigger emergency regulatory responses. The system does not avoid incoherence; it develops the capacity to hold incoherence without fragmenting, which is the precondition for integration.

The Consciousness paper's treatment of contemplative states (Section 10.3) analyzes advanced meditation as involving changes in the self-modeling dimension of coherence: the practitioner systematically relaxes the self-referential constraints that normally organize experience around an ego-center, producing states of expanded unity and reduced self-other boundary. In the psychological domain, this corresponds to the developmental progression toward integrated coherence (Appendix F, Profile 5) — the capacity to maintain coherence without rigid identity defense.

Ritual and communal practices modulate coherence at the interpersonal level. Synchronous movement, shared chanting, collective mourning, and celebratory gatherings produce entrainment — the alignment of affective and physiological states across individuals — that strengthens the shared coherence field (CU-Ψ12) and reduces individual regulatory burden. This explains why isolation is so psychologically costly: it removes the distributed coherence infrastructure that most humans depend on for baseline regulation.

Physical exercise modulates coherence at the physiological base. Regular exercise reduces baseline norepinephrine reactivity (Appendix C, §C.4), stabilizes serotonergic regulation (Appendix C, §C.3), and improves the excitation-inhibition balance (Appendix C, §C.5) that underlies all higher-level integration. Its effectiveness as an intervention for depression and anxiety is well documented (Blumenthal et al., 2007; Schuch et al., 2016) and follows directly from the CU framework: by restoring physiological coherence at the regulatory base, exercise provides the foundation upon which higher-level integration can proceed.

Artistic and creative practices modulate coherence by providing structured contexts for integration — frameworks within which fragmented experience can be organized without the pressure of explicit self-examination. Writing, painting, music-making, and narrative construction allow the system to process and integrate material that may be too threatening or too diffuse for direct therapeutic engagement. The meaning map is revised not through confrontation but through creative reorganization — a parallel pathway to the insight produced by psychodynamic therapy, operating through expression rather than interpretation.

8.6 Why Therapeutic Change Is Nonlinear

A clinical observation that puzzles both therapists and patients is that therapeutic change is often nonlinear. Improvement does not follow a steady upward trajectory. Instead, periods of stability alternate with periods of increased distress, apparent regression, or confusion. Patients sometimes feel worse before they feel better. Familiar identity structures may dissolve before new ones consolidate.

The coherence framework makes this nonlinearity structurally intelligible. Genuine coherence reorganization — the transition from one attractor basin to another — requires passing through a region of the coherence landscape that is lower than both the current basin and the target basin. In formal terms, the system must cross a separatrix — the ridge between attractor basins — and during the crossing, coherence temporarily decreases. This is experienced as increased distress, confusion, identity uncertainty, or vulnerability.

This is why premature stabilization is a therapeutic risk. When the discomfort of transition triggers emergency responses — from the patient, the therapist, or the system's social environment — the system may be pulled back into its original attractor basin before the transition is complete. The distress is interpreted as evidence that things are going wrong, when in fact it is evidence that the system is moving through the structurally necessary phase of reorganization. Attempts to eliminate discomfort at this stage preserve surface stability at the cost of deeper repair.

Effective therapy requires the capacity to distinguish between destabilization that signals productive reorganization (temporary increase in D(u) during basin transition) and destabilization that signals genuine decompensation (the system approaching the boundary of V). The difference is not always obvious from the surface presentation — both involve increased distress. Clinical judgment, therapeutic alliance, and careful monitoring of the system's overall regulatory capacity are what make the distinction possible.

8.7 The Therapeutic Stance

If therapy is coherence modulation, then the therapeutic stance that CU implies is neither the medical model (diagnosis and targeted intervention) nor the humanistic model (unconditional positive regard and self-actualization) alone, though it incorporates elements of both.

The CU therapist understands the patient as a coherence-maintaining system that has encountered conditions exceeding its regulatory capacity — or that has adopted compensatory strategies whose local success produces global costs. The symptoms are not random, meaningless, or merely neurochemical; they are the system's best available response to its coherence situation. Understanding them requires understanding the landscape — the meaning map, the attractor structure, the IES load, the identity constraints — not merely cataloging the surface features.

The therapist's role is to support the system's inherent drive toward viable coherence (CU-D2, CU-D3). When conditions are right — safety, attunement, time, and appropriate constraint — psychological systems reorganize toward greater integration on their own. The therapist does not impose coherence from outside; she provides the conditions within which the system's own coherence drive can operate effectively.

This means that the therapeutic question is never simply "What is wrong?" but always "What would support reintegration?" — which may involve insight, behavioral change, pharmacological support, environmental modification, relational repair, somatic work, creative expression, or some combination, depending on where coherence has failed and what the system needs to repair it.

With this applied framework in place — the understanding that all effective intervention modulates coherence, that different modalities target different layers, and that change requires temporary destabilization before restabilization — we can extend the analysis beyond the individual, examining how coherence operates in the value systems, political beliefs, and meaning structures that organize collective life.

This section has analyzed therapy, healing practices, and psychoactive substances as coherence interventions — diverse modalities unified by their effect on the system's integrative capacity. Effective intervention modulates coherence across timescales: immediate stabilization, medium-term integration, and long-term developmental trajectory change. The CU framework provides a principled basis for evaluating which interventions serve genuine repair and which substitute one form of incoherence for another.

Section 9: Moral, Political, and Meaning Systems — Coherence in Value Space

Moral beliefs, political ideologies, and meaning systems are often treated as separate from psychology proper — belonging to philosophy, sociology, or political theory. From the perspective of Coherence Universalism, this separation is artificial. These systems play a central psychological role: they organize the evaluative dimension of meaning space, enabling individuals and groups to maintain coherence across uncertainty, conflict, and long time horizons. They are not add-ons to psychological functioning; they are among its most consequential structures.

This section addresses a range of Coherence Ladder rungs that extend from individual meaning (Rung 21) through social norms and institutions (Rungs 24–26) into the normative domain proper (Rungs 27–30). Rung 27 (Value Differentiation) establishes that not all stable coherence is desirable — some forms systematically destroy coherence elsewhere or in the future. Rung 28 (Harm Detection) establishes that harm is the destruction or degradation of coherence across agents or time. Rung 29 (Tradeoff Resolution) establishes that coherence demands often conflict and that ethical reasoning manages these conflicts. Rung 30 (Norm Justification) establishes that norms must be defended with reasons that generalize beyond immediate interests.

These rungs are not abstract philosophical landmarks. They describe psychological capacities that develop (or fail to develop) in individual minds, that are scaffolded (or undermined) by social institutions, and whose failure produces characteristic forms of psychological and collective suffering. This section treats them as psychological realities before they become ethical prescriptions.

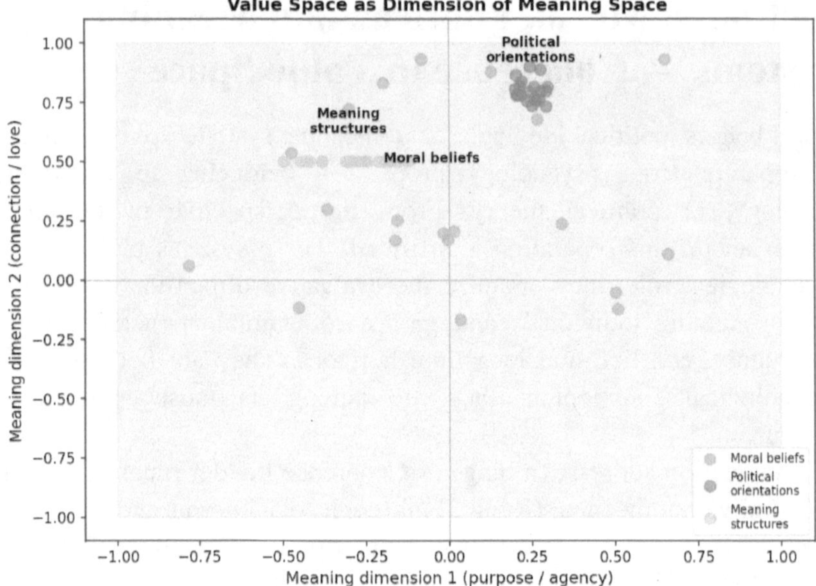

Figure 11. *Value space as a dimension of meaning space. Moral beliefs, political orientations, and meaning structures occupy distinct but coupled regions of the psychological meaning map, with coherence constraints operating across all three simultaneously.*

9.1 Value Space as a Dimension of Meaning Space

Value space is the structured region of meaning space M (CU-Ψ1) in which judgments about right and wrong, good and bad, permissible and forbidden are organized. Like the perceptual and cognitive dimensions of M, value space must be coherent for action to be possible at all. An agent cannot deliberate, commit, or coordinate without some stable evaluative structure — some way of distinguishing actions that support coherence from actions that degrade it.

This is not a metaphor. Neuropsychological evidence (Damasio, 1994; Greene, 2013) demonstrates that damage to the neural substrates of moral evaluation — particularly ventromedial prefrontal cortex — produces not merely different moral judgments but the collapse of evaluative capacity itself. The patient does not adopt new values; he loses the ability to organize action around values at all. In CU terms, the value dimension of M has been damaged, and the system can no longer navigate the evaluative landscape that moral action requires.

Value space, like meaning space more broadly, is not fixed. It is shaped by development, culture, attachment history, and the specific demands of the system's environment. What varies across individuals and cultures is not the structural requirement for evaluative coherence (which is universal) but the specific configuration of value space — which commitments occupy central positions, which tradeoffs are prioritized, and which regions of value space are navigated with confidence versus avoided or suppressed.

9.2 Moral Beliefs as Coherence Constraints

Moral beliefs function as coherence constraints within value space. They reduce the complexity of decision-making by ruling out classes of actions that would destabilize identity, relationships, or social trust. In this sense, morality is not primarily a set of abstract rules or rational principles. It is a psychological technology for preserving coherence across agents and over time.

This psychological account does not reduce morality to mere instrumental calculation. CU's foundational argument — developed in the Introduction and extended in CU — Ethics — is that moral structure is discovered at the limit of coherent explanation, not invented by individual or collective preference. The psychological claim here is more modest and more empirically grounded: whatever the ultimate status of moral truths, moral beliefs function within psychological systems as coherence constraints that organize the evaluative landscape and make coordinated action possible.

Haidt's (2001, 2012) moral foundations theory provides empirical support for this structural view. Haidt identifies five (later six) moral foundations — care/harm, fairness/cheating, loyalty/betrayal, authority/subversion, sanctity/degradation, and liberty/oppression — that recur across cultures. From a CU perspective, these foundations are not arbitrary psychological modules but dimensions of the coherence landscape along which moral evaluation operates. Each foundation tracks a specific kind of coherence threat: harm threatens the coherence of agents; cheating threatens the coherence of cooperative systems; betrayal threatens the coherence of group bonds; subversion threatens the coherence of hierarchical coordination; degradation threatens the coherence of identity boundaries; oppression threatens the coherence of autonomous agency.

The cross-cultural recurrence of these dimensions reflects the universality of the coherence challenges they address. The variation in how different cultures weight them reflects the fact that different environments, histories, and social structures make different dimensions most salient. Liberal moral systems tend to weight care and fairness most heavily; conservative moral systems distribute weight more evenly across all foundations. CU interprets this not as evidence that one weighting is correct and the other mistaken, but as evidence that different social environments produce different coherence landscapes in which different dimensions are most pressing.

Kohlberg's (1981) developmental model of moral reasoning can be similarly reframed. Kohlberg's stages — from pre-conventional (punishment avoidance, self-interest) through conventional (social conformity, law and order) to post-conventional (social contract, universal principles) — describe a progression in the scope and depth of coherence that moral reasoning can integrate. At each stage, the system can sustain moral coherence across a wider range of agents, timescales, and competing demands. This maps directly onto the Ladder's progression from Rung 24 (Norm Formation — locally stabilized behavioral expectations) through Rung 30 (Norm Justification — reasons that generalize beyond immediate interests). It also maps onto the attractor dynamics developed in Appendix G: moral reasoning capacity depends on the system's deepest attractor, and systems regulated by social approval (Profile 2) reason differently than systems regulated by epistemic coherence (Profile 4) — not because they are morally inferior but because their coherence landscapes have different shapes.

9.3 Political Beliefs as Scaled Coherence Strategies

Political beliefs operate at a larger scale than personal moral commitments, extending coherence across groups. Ideologies simplify complex social realities, providing narratives that coordinate behavior, justify institutional arrangements, and distribute resources in ways that maintain collective coherence — at least for the groups whose interests the ideology primarily serves.

When functioning well, political ideologies reduce coordination costs and enable collective action. A shared ideological framework provides the evaluative scaffolding that makes large-scale cooperation possible: it tells participants what matters, who to trust, what counts as progress, and how to interpret ambiguous situations. In CU terms, ideology extends the shared coherence field (CU-Ψ12) from the interpersonal scale of Section 6 to the institutional scale of Rungs 25–26.

When ideologies become rigid or totalizing, they exhibit the same local—global tension (CU-Ψ6) that operates throughout psychology, now at collective scale. Strong ideological commitment preserves local coherence — shared narratives, moral certainty, group loyalty, clear boundaries between us and them — while often degrading global coherence across society. The in-group achieves high FCS (CU-Ψ3) at the cost of escalating distortion D(u) in its relationship with out-groups, with reality, and with the complexity of the problems it faces.

This dynamic is visible across the political spectrum. Ideological rigidity on the left produces purity tests, suppression of internal dissent, and progressive narrowing of acceptable discourse — each iteration preserving group coherence while reducing the system's capacity to engage with perspectives that do not conform to its evaluative framework. Ideological rigidity on the right produces parallel dynamics with different content: loyalty demands, authority reinforcement, and boundary hardening that preserve traditional coherence structures while resisting the integration of new information or changed conditions. In both cases, the structural pattern is identical: local coherence is maintained through escalating exclusion, producing a feedback loop in which the group's meaning map becomes increasingly distorted relative to the territory it purports to represent.

Polarization is therefore not a failure of rationality but a coherence phenomenon. When coherence challenges intensify — economic disruption, cultural change, institutional failure, information overload — groups respond by narrowing their coherence boundaries and intensifying internal alignment. This produces the paradox of contemporary political life: the more uncertain and complex the environment becomes, the more rigidly groups cling to simplified narratives that cannot accommodate that complexity. The simplification maintains group coherence; the inability to accommodate complexity degrades adaptive capacity. The system stabilizes locally while becoming increasingly fragile globally.

9.4 Meaning as Long-Horizon Coherence

Meaning systems integrate moral and political values into broader narratives about purpose, history, and identity. They answer not only "What should I do?" but "Who am I?" and "What is this all for?" Meaning is not an abstract luxury layered onto basic psychological functioning. As established in Section 4.6, it is the longest-horizon coherence signal — the felt assessment of whether values, identity, and future orientation are integrated into a sustainable structure.

This corresponds to Rung 21 (Meaning) on the Coherence Ladder: the point at which coherence becomes not merely maintained but significant — where the system's trajectory acquires direction, purpose, and evaluative weight that extends beyond immediate needs. Meaning stabilizes motivation when immediate rewards are insufficient (explaining why Fra nkl's [1946] concentration camp survivors endured through meaning whe n every immediate gradient pointed toward despair). Meaning sustains coherence when outcomes are uncertain or delayed (explaining why people endure years of difficult training, unrewarding labor, or painful growth for the sake of a long-horizon vision that organizes their present action).

The collapse of meaning — the loss of the longest-horizon coherence structure — is among the most psychologically devastating events a person can experience, as developed in Section 4.5's analysis of depression. But meaning collapse also operates at collective scales, producing civilizational consequences that are inseparable from their individual psychological manifestations. Durkheim's (1897) concept of anomie — the collapse of social norms and their regulatory function — describes, in CU terms, the degradation of shared meaning structures at the institutional level, producing a population-level increase in IES that manifests as increased suicide, substance use, and social fragmentation. The "deaths of despair" documented by Case and Deaton (2015, 2020) — deaths from suicide, drug overdose, and alcoholic liver disease concentrated in communities that have lost economic purpose and social coherence — are the contemporary expression of anomie, measurable in mortality data.

9.5 Self-Deception in Moral and Political Reasoning

Self-deception (CU-Ψ11), developed in Section 5.5 as a general identity-protection mechanism, takes on particular significance in the moral and political domains because the stakes of coherence maintenance are so high and the costs of honest integration so visible.

When certain moral facts or political implications cannot be integrated without undermining identity coherence, agents distort their meaning maps — selectively attending to evidence, rationalizing contradictions, reinterpreting inconvenient data, or attributing their opponents' positions to bad faith rather than engaging with their content. These strategies preserve local coherence (the agent's self-model as a moral person remains intact) while degrading global coherence (the agent's relationship to reality, to out-groups, and to the complexity of the moral situation deteriorates).

The CU analysis of moral self-deception is precise: it occurs when the value dimension of the meaning map Φ is distorted so that morally threatening information falls outside the region of M that the system navigates. The person who benefits from an unjust system but cannot integrate that fact without destabilizing her self-model as a good person does not lack the information; she lacks the coherence capacity to integrate it. The meaning map is adjusted so that the unjust benefit is invisible, reinterpreted as earned, or attributed to structural forces beyond her control. Each adjustment increases distortion D(u) while preserving local FCS.

This is not an excuse for moral failure — it is a structural explanation with direct implications for how moral failure should be addressed. Moral critique that attacks the self-model without providing a path to integration will be experienced as a coherence threat and will produce defensive self-deception rather than moral growth. Effective moral persuasion must provide the evaluative scaffolding within which the threatening truth can be integrated — just as effective therapy provides the relational safety within which traumatic material can be processed. The ethical implications of this insight are developed extensively in CU — Ethics.

9.6 Relativism, Objectivity, and the Viability Criterion

This section's analysis raises the question that CU's moral framework addresses head-on: if moral and political systems vary because coherence constraints vary across contexts, does this imply moral relativism?

CU's answer, developed at length in the Introduction and in CU — Ethics, is no — but the reason is structural rather than foundational. Moral systems vary, but not all systems are equally viable. Those that systematically disable agency, suppress integration, require escalating self-deception, or destroy coherence in neighboring systems tend to collapse or produce cascading harm over time. The criterion is not consensus, tradition, or intuitive appeal. It is viability — the capacity of the moral system to sustain coherence across agents and timescales without progressive degradation.

This is the psychological dimension of a claim that CU makes at every scale: coherence is discovered, not invented, at the limit of explanation. In the psychological domain, this means that a person's moral beliefs are not arbitrary preferences but coherence constraints that either support or undermine her capacity for integrated functioning across value space. Beliefs that require systematic self-deception to maintain are less viable than beliefs that can withstand honest scrutiny — not because honesty is an arbitrary value but because self-deception produces escalating distortion that eventually undermines agency itself.

The viability criterion does not settle every moral dispute. It does not tell a person whether to be a consequentialist or a deontologist, whether to value individual liberty over collective welfare, or how to weight competing moral foundations. What it does is constrain the space of viable moral positions: positions that require the systematic destruction of coherence — in the agent, in other agents, or in the systems that support coherence at larger scales — fall outside the viable region, regardless of how locally coherent they appear to their adherents.

9.7 The Connection Between Psychological and Moral Health

Psychological health at the individual level and moral health at the collective level are deeply connected — more deeply than either psychology or moral philosophy typically acknowledges.

Both depend on maintaining coherence in value space without rigidifying into dogma or dissolving into incoherence. The psychologically healthy individual can hold moral complexity without fragmentation, revise moral commitments when evidence demands it, and act coherently across competing evaluative demands. The morally healthy society can sustain shared evaluative frameworks without suppressing dissent, accommodate moral diversity without abandoning evaluative standards, and navigate tradeoffs without sacrificing the coherence of its most vulnerable members.

The connection is not merely analogical. It is structural. The same coherence dynamics that produce anxiety, depression, and self-deception in individual psychological systems produce polarization, institutional corruption, and collective self-deception in social systems. The same local—global tension (CU-Ψ6) that makes individual coherence difficult makes collective coherence difficult. The same attractor dynamics (Appendix F) that shape individual moral reasoning shape collective moral culture. And the same therapeutic insight — that genuine integration requires temporary destabilization, that premature closure prevents deeper coherence, that the system's own coherence drive will guide reorganization if the conditions are right — applies at collective scales as surely as at individual ones.

This structural continuity is what makes the CU psychology paper a necessary precursor to CU — Ethics. Without understanding how coherence operates within individual psychological systems — how moral beliefs function as coherence constraints, how self-deception distorts moral reasoning, how attractor dynamics shape moral development — the ethical framework lacks its psychological foundation. And without the ethical framework, the psychological analysis remains incomplete: it can describe how moral systems function but cannot yet assess which moral configurations are viable in the fullest sense.

This section has shown that moral reasoning, political judgment, and meaning-making are coherence phenomena — not separate cognitive faculties but expressions of the system's capacity for justificatory integration. Self-deception (CU-Ψ11) is the central failure mode, operating identically in moral, political, and existential domains. This structural continuity makes the Psychology paper a necessary precursor to CU — Ethics.

Section 10: Group Psychology, Culture, and Religion — Shared Coherence Fields

Psychological coherence does not reside solely within individual minds. Human cognition is irreducibly social, and many of the structures that stabilize experience, identity, and meaning are distributed across groups. From families and communities to nations and civilizations, groups function as systems that coordinate belief, behavior, and value across many agents simultaneously. Understanding how they do so — and how they fail — requires extending the coherence framework from the individual to the collective.

This section formalizes that extension.

CU-Ψ12. Shared Coherence Fields. A shared coherence field is a distributed regulatory structure in which multiple agents' coherence is jointly maintained through coordinated representations, norms, practices, and narrative. Individual coherence within the field depends partly on the field's stability; the field's stability depends partly on individual participation. Neither level is reducible to the other.

Shared coherence fields correspond to the Coherence Ladder's social rungs: Rung 22 (Shared Representations) establishes that coherence can be distributed across agents through language, symbols, and practices. Rung 23 (Coordination Dynamics) establishes that social order arises from mutual prediction, feedback, and alignment — not external imposition. Rung 24 (Norm Formation) establishes that stabilized coordination patterns become expected and function as attractors in social coherence space. Rung 25 (Institutions) establishes that norms can be formalized and enforced across time and scale. Rung 26 (Culture) establishes that high-level coherence can persist across generations through shared narratives, practices, and values — that culture is the memory of social systems.

This section traces these rungs through their psychological manifestations: group dynamics, cultural systems, and religious traditions.

10.1 Group Coherence as Distributed Regulation

The fundamental insight of group psychology, from CU's perspective, is that belonging to a group reduces the burden of individual coherence maintenance. When a person participates in a shared coherence field, expectations are clarified, roles are defined, uncertainty is constrained, and the regulatory load of navigating meaning space is distributed across multiple agents. This is not a weakness of human psychology. It is a structural necessity. No individual can maintain global coherence alone.

The empirical evidence for this claim is extensive. Baumeister and Leary (1995) identify belongingness as a fundamental human motivation — not because humans merely prefer company but because social exclusion produces measurable physiological dysregulation, cognitive impairment, and increased mortality risk (Cacioppo & Hawkley, 2009; Holt-Lunstad et al., 2010). In CU terms, social exclusion contracts the system's effective viability region V by removing the distributed regulatory support on which coherence depends. The isolated system must self-regulate processes that were previously jointly regulated — the same mechanism that makes attachment loss devastating (Section 6.1), now operating at group scale.

This distributed quality of coherence explains why group membership feels stabilizing even when the group's beliefs are factually wrong or its practices are ethically questionable. The coherence benefit of belonging is not primarily epistemic (the group gives me true beliefs) but regulatory (the group shares my coherence burden). A person embedded in a tight-knit community with inaccurate beliefs about the world may function with higher FCS (CU-Ψ3) than an isolated individual with accurate beliefs, because the regulatory benefit of distributed coherence exceeds the epistemic cost of shared error — at least in the short and medium term. The long-term costs of shared distortion are real (Section 9.5), but they accumulate slowly, while the regulatory benefits of belonging are immediate and substantial.

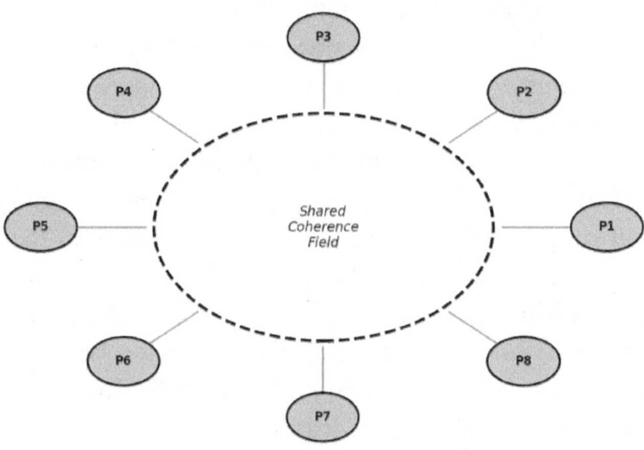

Figure 12. *Shared coherence fields. Individual nodes (circles) are connected by coherence links whose strength reflects mutual regulatory influence. The central dashed circle represents the shared coherence field — the emergent structure that culture, ritual, narrative, and shared meaning sustain across a group. Group coherence is not reducible to the sum of individual coherence levels; it is an emergent property of the coupling structure.*

10.2 Classic Group Phenomena Reframed

The major findings of social psychology — conformity, obedience, groupthink, deindividuation, social facilitation — can be systematically reframed as coherence dynamics operating at the group level.

Conformity. Asch's (1951) conformity experiments demonstrated that individuals will report obviously incorrect perceptual judgments when a unanimous majority reports those judgments. The standard interpretation emphasizes social pressure and the desire to fit in. CU adds a structural dimension: the unanimous majority constitutes a shared coherence field that the individual must either join or resist. Resisting means maintaining individual perceptual coherence at the cost of interpersonal coherence — the system must tolerate the IES of standing alone against a unanimous group, which is not merely uncomfortable but constitutes a genuine coherence threat at the social dimension of meaning space.

Conformity is not irrationality; it is CU-Ψ6 operating between perceptual and social coherence, with the social dimension winning because its regulatory consequences are more immediate and more severe.

Obedience. Milgram's (1963) obedience experiments demonstrated that ordinary people will administer apparently dangerous electric shocks under the authority of an experimenter. CU interprets this not as moral weakness but as coherence capture: the experimental context constitutes a coherence field (the authority of science, the structure of the experimental situation, the social contract of participation) that is powerful enough to override the individual's moral coherence. The participant does not stop caring about the victim; he cannot integrate his moral concern with the coherence demands of the situation without destabilizing the entire framework that makes his behavior intelligible. The authority structure provides coherence; disobedience would produce a coherence crisis (What is happening? Who am I? What do the rules mean?) that the system is not prepared to navigate.

Groupthink. Janis's (1972) analysis of catastrophic group decision-making — the Bay of Pigs invasion, the Challenger disaster — demonstrates that groups can maintain high internal coherence while making decisions that are globally disastrous. In CU terms, groupthink is CU-Ψ6 at collective scale: the group optimizes for internal alignment (local coherence) by suppressing dissent, filtering contradictory information, and maintaining an illusion of unanimity — all of which preserve the shared coherence field while degrading the group's relationship with reality. The group's FCS remains high within its own meaning map while its meaning map becomes increasingly distorted relative to the territory.

Deindividuation. Le Bon (1895) observed that individuals in crowds often behave in ways they would not behave alone — with reduced self-awareness, heightened emotional intensity, and diminished individual responsibility. CU interprets deindividuation as a shift in attractor dominance: the individual's self-referential coherence (CU-I4) is partially absorbed into the group's shared coherence field. Individual meaning-map constraints are relaxed as the group's regulatory field becomes dominant. This can produce both destructive behavior (mob violence, riot) and constructive behavior (collective ecstasy, ritual solidarity, the shared coherence of a protest movement that feels larger than any individual). The mechanism is the same: the locus of coherence maintenance shifts from the individual to the collective, with consequences that depend entirely on the content and structure of the collective field.

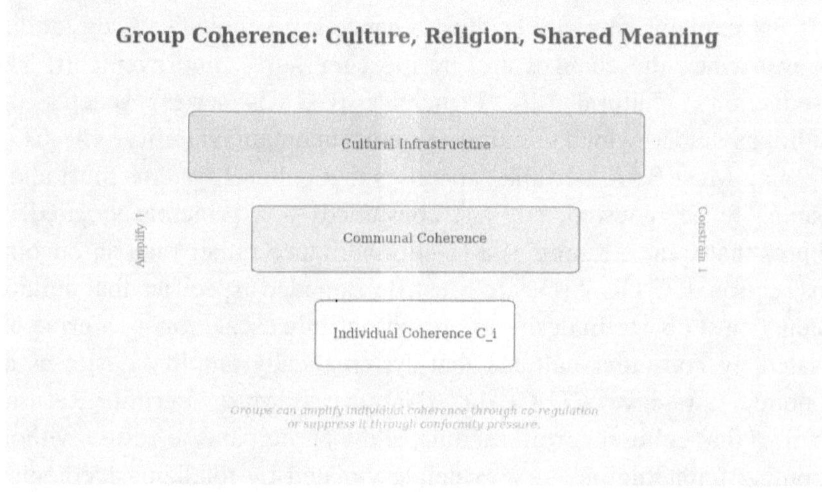

Figure 13. Culture and religion as coherence technologies. Temporal depth (narrative continuity), social binding (shared ritual and meaning), and existential anchoring (cosmological framing) represent three dimensions of long-horizon coherence maintenance.

10.3 Culture as Collective Coherence Memory

Culture functions as collective memory and pattern storage — the repository of solutions to recurring coordination problems encoded in language, ritual, law, art, and custom. Cultural practices persist not because they are always optimal but because they have historically maintained coherence under specific conditions. Culture is, in the precise sense of Rung 26, the memory of social systems — the mechanism by which coherence strategies outlive the individuals who developed them.

This functional account explains several features of culture that are otherwise puzzling. It explains cultural conservatism: practices persist because they encode coherence solutions, and discarding them without replacement increases collective IES. It explains cultural variation: different environments produce different coherence challenges, and different cultures develop different strategies for meeting them. It explains cultural rigidity under threat: when environmental change threatens existing coherence structures, cultures often respond by intensifying traditional practices rather than innovating — because the familiar strategy is immediately available while alternatives are untested and therefore uncertain.

It also explains why rapid cultural change is psychologically destabilizing even when the changes are, by most measures, improvements. The Introduction's Cultural Life Principles (CU-CL series) specify the conditions under which cultural systems maintain viability. CU-CL-8 (Meaning Must Be Renewable) specifies that cultural systems must allow meaning to be renewed, not just consumed — a principle violated by cultures that treat meaning as a fixed inheritance rather than an ongoing construction. CU-CL-9 (Desire Must Be Bounded) specifies that cultural systems must constrain desire to prevent infinite escalation — a principle violated by consumer cultures that systematically amplify desire as an economic strategy. CU-CL-11 (Narratives Must Permit Refusal) specifies that cultural narratives must allow participants to refuse without becoming unintelligible — a principle violated by totalizing ideological systems (both religious and secular) that cannot accommodate internal dissent.

When these conditions are violated, culture ceases to function as a coherence support system and becomes a coherence extraction system — maintaining the appearance of collective stability while progressively degrading the coherence of the individuals within it. The psychological consequences are measurable: anomie, meaninglessness, rising anxiety and depression, substance use as self-medication for unmet coherence needs.

10.4 Religion as Long-Horizon Coherence Technology

Religion represents a particularly powerful class of shared coherence systems — arguably the most powerful that human cultures have developed. At their best, religious traditions integrate moral norms, cosmological narrative, ritual practice, identity formation, and community belonging into a single stabilizing structure that operates across generations.

The components of religious systems map directly onto coherence functions:

Ritual synchronizes bodies and attention across participants, producing the physiological and affective entrainment described in Section 8.5 — the alignment of regulatory states that strengthens the shared coherence field and reduces individual regulatory burden. Durkheim's (1912) concept of collective effervescence — the heightened emotional energy produced by communal ritual — is, in CU terms, the felt registration of increased shared coherence: the individual experiences the field's regulatory power as elevation, connection, and meaning that transcends individual capacity.

Myth and narrative organize meaning at scales too large for individual experience. Creation narratives, eschatological visions, and sacred histories provide the longest-horizon coherence structures available to human psychology — frameworks that situate individual suffering, purpose, and action within a cosmic context. These narratives operate at the meaning level (Rung 21) by connecting individual life to something larger, which is why religious meaning-loss is among the most psychologically destabilizing forms of meaning collapse (Section 4.6, Section 9.4).

Ethical codes constrain behavior in ways that preserve trust, cooperation, and social coherence across time. They function as the normative dimension (Rungs 24, 27–30) of the shared coherence field, specifying which actions are compatible with collective viability and which threaten it. The persistence of strikingly similar ethical principles across unrelated religious traditions — prohibitions on murder, theft, deception, and betrayal — reflects the universality of the coherence challenges these principles address.

Community provides the distributed regulatory infrastructure within which all other religious functions operate. Religious belonging is not an add-on to religious belief; it is the social substrate through which religious coherence is maintained and transmitted. Belief without community is cognitively fragile; community without belief is motivationally shallow. The integration of the two is what gives religion its distinctive psychological power.

From a CU perspective, religion is neither reducible to superstition nor automatically authoritative. It is a long-horizon coherence technology — one that can succeed or fail depending on how it balances the competing demands of stability and adaptation, internal coherence and external accuracy, collective alignment and individual integrity.

The Introduction's Transcendental Orientation Principles (CU-T series) specify the evaluative framework. CU-T-3 (Permissible Metaphysical Postures) permits multiple metaphysical orientations — theistic, non-theistic, agnostic — without endorsing any, because what matters for coherence is not doctrine but structural function. CU-T-4 (What CU Explicitly Rejects) rejects spiritual systems that violate coherence constraints: those that require self-deception, demand the destruction of local coherence, or claim access to truth that bypasses constraint. CU-T-7 (Faith Reinterpreted) reframes faith not as belief without evidence but as sustained commitment to coherence under uncertainty. CU-T-5 (The Sacred Reframed) redefines the sacred as the fact that coherence matters and its destruction calls for repair — not mysticism but structural observation. CU-T-6 (Practice, Prayer, and Ritual) evaluates spiritual practices by their effects on coherence: practices that preserve and extend coherence are legitimate; those that fragment it are not.

When religious systems become rigid, exclusionary, or immune to revision, they exhibit the same CU-Ψ6 dynamics visible in political ideology (Section 9.3): they preserve in-group coherence at the cost of broader social integration, maintain the shared field's internal FCS while progressively distorting its relationship to reality. The system's self-deception (CU-Ψ11) becomes collective: inconvenient evidence is suppressed, dissent is framed as betrayal, and the group's meaning map narrows to exclude any information that would require revision of the founding narrative. The result is a community that feels deeply meaningful to its members while becoming increasingly disconnected from the world it inhabits — a configuration that can persist for generations but is ultimately fragile, because the gap between map and territory accumulates costs that eventually become undeniable.

10.5 Radicalization as Coherence Capture

The dynamics of radicalization — whether religious, political, or ideological — become structurally intelligible through the shared coherence field framework.

Radicalization typically begins with a coherence crisis. The individual's existing meaning structure has failed — through trauma, social marginalization, identity confusion, loss of purpose, or cultural dislocation. IES is elevated; navigable gradients are absent; the system is in the depressive configuration described in Section 4.5 — registering that something is profoundly wrong but perceiving no viable path forward.

The radicalizing group offers a solution to this crisis. It provides a comprehensive shared coherence field: a clear narrative that explains the individual's suffering, identifies its cause, specifies the enemy, and offers a path to meaning, purpose, and belonging. The group's coherence field is powerful precisely because it is simple, total, and demanding. It resolves the individual's coherence crisis rapidly and completely by absorbing individual regulation into the collective field. In exchange, the individual surrenders individual coherence maintenance — the capacity for independent evaluation, dissent, and self-referential constraint enforcement (CU-I4) — to the group.

This exchange explains why radicalization is so resistant to factual correction. The radical's beliefs are not held because they are evidentially supported; they are held because they are coherence-maintaining. Challenging the beliefs threatens to reopen the coherence crisis that the group resolved — to return the individual to the intolerable state of meaninglessness, isolation, and directionless suffering that preceded radicalization. The beliefs are therefore defended not as propositions but as identity — because they function as identity-level coherence constraints, and their abandonment would constitute identity collapse (CU-I5).

De-radicalization, consequently, cannot succeed through argumentation alone. It requires providing an alternative coherence field — an alternative source of meaning, belonging, purpose, and identity — that is compelling enough to replace the one the radical group provides. Without such an alternative, de-radicalization asks the individual to abandon coherence for incoherence, which no coherence-maintaining system will do voluntarily.

10.6 The Dual Nature of Shared Coherence

Shared coherence is both enabling and constraining — and the tension between these functions is irreducible.

Enabling: shared coherence fields allow individuals to act with confidence, purpose, and meaning. They reduce regulatory load, provide evaluative frameworks, stabilize identity, and extend the scope of coordinated action far beyond individual capacity. Human civilization is, in its entirety, the product of shared coherence — of the capacity to build and maintain collective meaning structures that outlive individual agents and accumulate coherence solutions across generations.

Constraining: shared coherence fields also suppress dissent, inhibit integration of new information, and punish deviation from group norms. They can trap individuals in coherence configurations that are locally functional but globally maladaptive — configurations that maintain the group's internal stability at the cost of individual autonomy, epistemic integrity, or moral development. The pressure to maintain shared coherence can prevent the very transitions that individual development (Section 5.4, Appendix F) requires.

Healthy cultures balance stability with openness — allowing coherence structures to evolve rather than calcify. They permit the renewal of meaning (CU-CL-8) without abandoning the structures that make meaning possible. They tolerate internal dissent (CU-CL-11) without dissolving into fragmentation. They maintain collective identity without requiring individual self-deception.

This balance is difficult to achieve and impossible to guarantee. Every culture, every institution, every shared coherence field faces the fundamental tradeoff between internal alignment and adaptive flexibility — between the coherence that comes from agreement and the coherence that comes from honest engagement with disagreement. The cultures that persist longest are typically those that have found ways to institutionalize both: to maintain strong shared identity while creating protected spaces for dissent, revision, and innovation. But even the most adaptive cultures can become rigid under sufficient stress, and even the most rigid cultures can be reformed under sufficient pressure.

10.7 Social Breakdown as Coherence Crisis

Understanding groups as shared coherence fields clarifies why social breakdown is psychologically devastating in ways that transcend any individual's circumstances.

Loss of cultural narratives, erosion of institutional trust, and fragmentation of shared meaning dramatically increase the regulatory burden on individuals. The distributed coherence infrastructure that most people depend on for baseline regulation — the shared frameworks that make sense of work, family, citizenship, and purpose — degrades, and each person must now self-regulate processes that were previously collectively maintained. Individual IES spikes not because individual conditions have necessarily worsened but because collective coherence support has been withdrawn.

10.7.1 From Individual Trauma to Collective Dynamics

Section 7.2.9 established the mechanism by which individual trauma propagates socially: self-deception stabilizes constrained regimes, constrained regimes externalize harm, and harm generates new trauma in others. At the collective scale, this individual mechanism produces emergent dynamics that are not reducible to the psychology of any single agent.

When large numbers of individuals operate within restricted viability regions — whether because of widespread trauma, economic precarity, or cultural dislocation — the collective viable region contracts. A group of agents each operating within narrow constraint spaces must find shared narratives that are stable for all participants. As the participants' individual viability regions shrink, the intersection of those regions shrinks faster. The group can no longer stabilize around nuanced or reality-tracking models, because those models require psychological states that some members cannot maintain. The group instead stabilizes around simplified, emotionally safe attractors.

These constrained group attractors have predictable properties: binary moral framing, identity-protective reasoning, outgroup attribution of threat, resistance to disconfirming evidence, and moral certainty with low predictive accuracy. These are not communication failures — they are stability equilibria. The group has found the simplest shared coherence configuration that its members can collectively maintain, and it defends that configuration against any perturbation.

10.7.2 Polarization as Competing Coherence Regimes

When multiple groups stabilize around incompatible defensive attractors, mutual correction becomes destabilizing rather than informative. Interaction between groups no longer transmits information — it transmits threat. Each group experiences the other not as mistaken but as reality-destroying, because the other group's claims, if true, would force regime transitions that the members cannot survive without support.

Polarization is therefore not primarily disagreement about facts. It is the emergence of mutually exclusive coherence regimes — configurations that cannot coexist because each requires beliefs that would destabilize the other. The structural result is that the social system evolves toward stable separation: interaction produces destabilization, destabilization produces avoidance or hostility, and hostility further constrains each group's viable state space. Escalation becomes self-sustaining even when no individual actor desires it, because each defensive action constrains the other group's viability space further, producing reciprocal tightening in a positive feedback loop.

10.7.3 Economic Precarity and Coherence Capacity

The trauma cascade and polarization dynamics described above do not arise in a vacuum. They are typically triggered or amplified by material conditions — and the most important material condition, from a coherence perspective, is the availability of slack.

Coherence requires resources: cognitive, emotional, and temporal resources that allow a system to tolerate uncertainty while reorganizing. When survival pressure dominates attention, systems optimize for immediate stabilization rather than long-term integration. The mind under economic threat cannot afford exploratory reasoning because prediction error carries survival cost.

Material stress acts as a constraint operator on the system's viable interpretive space. Under scarcity, fewer interpretations remain stabilizable because ambiguity becomes dangerous. The consequences include intolerance of uncertainty, preference for simple causal stories, threat-sensitive cognition, reduced empathy bandwidth, and identity-protective reasoning. These are adaptive responses to volatility, not failures of intelligence.

When large populations experience this compression simultaneously, shared discourse collapses in complexity. The society shifts toward narratives that minimize cognitive load and emotional risk. Political radicalization therefore tracks perceived instability more reliably than ideology. Economic precarity does not merely produce dissatisfaction — it changes the kinds of beliefs a population can psychologically maintain.

The implications are substantial. Institutions that depend on long-horizon reasoning — science, law, democratic deliberation — require populations capable of tolerating uncertainty. When coherence capacity falls below a threshold, institutions must simplify to remain legible, and when they simplify they lose problem-solving capacity, which generates further precarity. This feedback cycle — precarity → reduced coherence capacity → institutional distrust → institutional degradation → more precarity — is the economic analogue of the individual trauma cascade, operating at social scale.

Economic security is therefore not merely a distributive concern. It is cognitive infrastructure: the material foundation required for shared truth-seeking and cooperative disagreement. Policies that reduce volatility increase collective epistemic capacity. Policies that increase volatility force societies toward simpler, conflict-prone attractors. The Social Dynamics paper develops this connection into a formal institutional design framework, treating economic stability as a precondition for the kind of collective coherence that democratic governance requires.

10.7.4 Implications: The Mental Health Crisis as a Social Coherence Crisis

What appears as a mental health crisis is often inseparable from a crisis of collective coherence. Appendix G (Modern Coherence Crisis) develops this argument in detail, but the core claim belongs here: the contemporary epidemic of anxiety, depression, meaninglessness, and social fragmentation cannot be understood solely through individual psychology. It reflects the degradation of shared coherence fields under conditions — informational overload, institutional failure, rapid cultural change, economic precarity, algorithmic optimization for engagement over integration — that exceed the adaptive capacity of coherence structures that evolved under radically different conditions.

This is not a counsel of despair. It is a diagnostic insight that shifts the target of intervention. Individual therapy remains necessary and valuable — the coherence of individual systems requires repair regardless of the social conditions that contributed to their damage. But individual therapy alone cannot restore the shared coherence infrastructure that collective life requires. Sustainable psychological health requires not only individual intervention but collective reorganization: the reconstruction of institutions, narratives, and practices that support coherence at the scale of communities, not merely the scale of individual minds.

The Social Dynamics paper takes up this challenge directly, developing a formal theory of social coherence attractors, institutional design principles, and the conditions under which societies can navigate collective regime transitions without collapse. The psychology paper's contribution is to establish the mechanisms — individual, interpersonal, and group — that such a social theory must respect.

This section has extended the framework from individual to group-level coherence dynamics: shared belief systems, cultural narratives, and religious institutions function as collective coherence infrastructure. Groups can amplify individual coherence through co-regulation or suppress it through conformity pressure. The Social Dynamics paper takes up this analysis at institutional and civilizational scales.

Section 11: Development, Evolution, and History — Coherence Across Time

Psychological coherence is not a static achievement. It is constructed, tested, revised, and sometimes lost across multiple temporal scales — from individual development to evolutionary history to the rise and collapse of civilizations. Viewing psychology through this extended temporal lens reveals coherence not only as a mechanism of moment-to-moment functioning but as a selection criterion operating across time at every scale.

This section is grounded in CU-D6 (The Multi-Timescale Coherence Principle): coherence is maintained across nested timescales, with faster dynamics constrained by slower integrative structures and slower structures emerging from accumulated faster processes. Individual development, evolutionary history, and civilizational change are not separate topics requiring separate explanatory frameworks. They are different temporal scales at which the same coherence dynamics operate — dynamics that produce, at each scale, the characteristic pattern of construction, testing, revision, and occasional catastrophic failure.

11.1 Development Across the Lifespan

Human psychological development can be understood as a progressive expansion of coherence capacity — the system's ability to maintain integrated regulation across an increasing number of domains, timescales, and levels of complexity.

11.1.1 From External to Internal Regulation

The developmental trajectory begins with near-total regulatory dependence. As established in Section 6.1, infants cannot maintain physiological or emotional coherence independently. Coherence is externally scaffolded: caregivers regulate arousal, modulate affect, structure attention, and provide the sensory predictability within which the infant's nervous system can begin constructing its own regulatory architecture.

Development proceeds through the progressive internalization of regulatory functions. Bowlby (1969) described this as the construction of internal working models — internalized representations of the attachment relationship that allow the child to self-regulate in the caregiver's absence. Vygotsky (1978) described the same process in the cognitive domain as the zone of proximal development: the child first performs cognitive tasks with adult scaffolding, then gradually internalizes the scaffolding until the task can be performed independently. In both cases, the structural pattern is identical: what was distributed coherence (maintained jointly by the child and an external regulator) becomes individual coherence (maintained by the child's own internal architecture).

Appendix F formalizes this trajectory as a progression through attractor dominance profiles. Profile 1 (External Attunement Dominant) describes the infant's complete dependence on external regulation. Profile 2 (Social Approval Dominant) describes the child's and early adolescent's organization around belonging, where the group — peers, family, school — replaces the individual caregiver as the primary external coherence scaffold. Profile 3 (Self-Image/Autonomy Dominant) describes the emergence of genuinely internal regulation, where the system begins to maintain coherence through self-referential constraint enforcement (CU-I4) rather than social approval alone. Profiles 4 and 5 describe progressively deeper forms of internal regulation — epistemic coherence dominance and integrated coherence — that emerge in some adults under favorable developmental conditions.

11.1.2 Developmental Milestones as Coherence Transitions

Developmental milestones — language acquisition, theory of mind, abstract reasoning, moral reasoning, identity formation — are not merely cognitive achievements. They mark shifts in the scale and complexity of coherence that the system can sustain. Each milestone expands the system's meaning space M, introducing new dimensions that must be integrated with existing ones.

Language acquisition (typically 12–36 months) dramatically expands the representational dimension of M, enabling the system to encode and communicate experiences that previously existed only as felt states. But language also introduces new coherence demands: the child must now integrate verbal and non-verbal experience, must maintain coherence between what she feels and what she can say, and must navigate the gap between private experience and shared representation. This gap — between the richness of experience and the compression of language — is a permanent source of coherence tension that every human system must manage.

Theory of mind (typically 3–5 years) introduces the social-modeling dimension of M. The child can now represent other agents' beliefs, desires, and intentions as distinct from her own. This capacity enables Rung 22 (Shared Representations) and Rung 23 (Coordination Dynamics) to operate psychologically: the child can participate in genuinely shared meaning rather than merely parallel activity. But it also introduces new coherence challenges — the management of deception, the negotiation of conflicting perspectives, and the recognition that others' meanings may be fundamentally different from one's own.

Adolescence is the most destabilizing developmental transition because coherence must be renegotiated across simultaneously changing domains. Bodily coherence is disrupted by puberty. Social coherence is disrupted by the shift from family to peer orientation. Identity coherence is disrupted by the need to construct a self-model that can sustain autonomous agency. Moral coherence is disrupted by the encounter with genuine moral complexity — the recognition that the rules that organized childhood may be inadequate for the dilemmas of adult life. The system must reorganize across all these dimensions concurrently, which is why adolescence is both a period of extraordinary vulnerability and extraordinary creative potential. The system is in transition between attractor basins (the separatrix-crossing described in Section 7.6), temporarily destabilized and therefore temporarily open to configurations that would be inaccessible from a stable adult state.

11.1.3 Development Does Not Eliminate Conflict

Healthy development does not eliminate conflict, tension, or vulnerability. It increases the system's ability to hold tension without fragmentation, to revise identity without collapse, and to act coherently across longer and more abstract horizons. This is what Section 5.8 describes as the expansion of integrative capacity — the direction of maturity.

Developmental failure often reflects not lack of intelligence or motivation but insufficient support for coherence during critical transitions. A child who does not receive adequate co-regulation during infancy may never develop the physiological foundation for affect tolerance. An adolescent whose individuation is punished by family or culture may arrest at Profile 2 (Social Approval Dominant) rather than developing internal regulation. An adult who never encounters conditions demanding identity revision may maintain a coherence strategy that is locally functional but globally brittle — adequate for stable environments, catastrophic under perturbation.

This is why developmental psychology and clinical psychology are inseparable from a CU perspective. Many presenting clinical problems are developmental in origin — not in the sense that they were "caused by childhood" in a simple linear way, but in the sense that the system's coherence architecture was shaped during development, and the current difficulties reflect the limitations of that architecture under present demands.

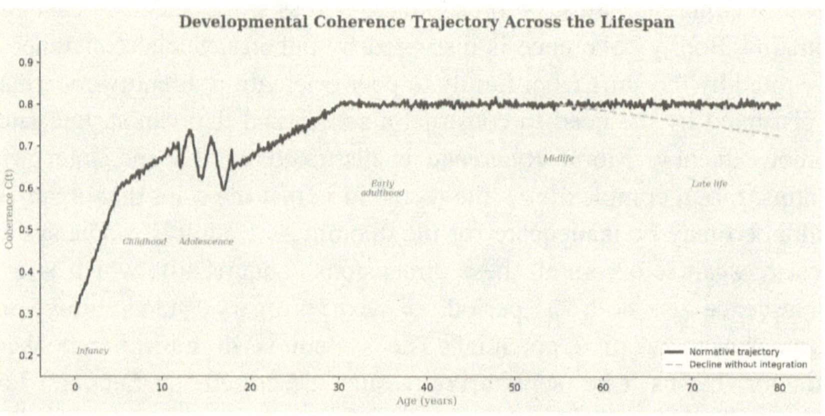

Figure 14. *Developmental coherence trajectory across the lifespan. Infancy shows rapid coherence growth as basic perceptual and regulatory structures form. Childhood shows steady growth. Adolescence introduces characteristic turbulence as identity structures reorganize. Adulthood represents a plateau with ongoing fluctuations. Late life may show gradual decline or, in cases of successful integration, sustained coherence. The trajectory is neither linear nor guaranteed: developmental crises, trauma, and environmental support all modulate the path.*

11.2 Evolutionary History

At the evolutionary scale, coherence functions as a selection pressure. Systems that cannot maintain integrated regulation over time do not persist. Biological evolution can therefore be understood, in part, as the exploration of increasingly complex coherence strategies — a progression that the Coherence Ladder traces from pure structure (Rung 1) through life (Rung 15) through consciousness (Rungs 16–21) to social and cultural organization (Rungs 22–26).

11.2.1 The Evolution of Coherence Architecture

Nervous systems evolved not simply to process information but to coordinate perception, action, and internal regulation in increasingly dynamic environments. The earliest nervous systems — diffuse nerve nets in cnidarians — achieved basic sensorimotor coherence: coordinated whole-body responses to stimuli. Centralized nervous systems — the evolutionary innovation of bilaterians — enabled more complex coherence: differentiated sensory processing, motor planning, and the beginning of internal modeling (Rung 16).

The evolution of vertebrate brains extended coherence along multiple dimensions simultaneously. Expanded cortical capacity enabled richer internal models. Limbic structures enabled affective regulation — the valence-based guidance system described in Section 3. Prefrontal elaboration enabled temporal extension — the capacity to maintain coherence across longer time horizons, to inhibit immediate responses in service of distal goals, and to construct the self-models that make identity-level coherence possible.

Social cognition evolved to extend coherence beyond the individual, enabling coordination, cooperation, and shared meaning — the Ladder's progression from Rung 22 through Rung 26. The evolution of language — arguably the most consequential cognitive development in the history of the biosphere — enabled the externalization and transmission of coherence strategies: solutions to coordination problems could now be encoded symbolically and transmitted across generations without requiring direct observation or imitation.

Cultural transmission amplified these effects exponentially, allowing coherence strategies to accumulate across generations in ways that genetic transmission alone could not support. CU-D7 (The Novelty Principle) specifies that adaptive novelty arises through navigation of structured coherence landscapes rather than random exploration alone. Cultural evolution instantiates this principle at the population level: each generation inherits not merely genetic constraints but an accumulated library of coherence strategies — tools, institutions, narratives, practices — that expand the navigable region of meaning space far beyond what any individual or generation could discover independently.

11.2.2 Evolution Does Not Optimize

A critical insight: evolution does not optimize for maximal coherence. It selects for viable coherence under specific environmental constraints. This distinction — between optimization and viability — has profound implications for understanding human psychology.

Human psychology contains tradeoffs, vulnerabilities, and failure modes that are not bugs but structural consequences of evolutionary history. The same mechanisms that enable creativity, abstraction, and moral concern also introduce fragility and susceptibility to breakdown. The capacity for temporal extension (Rung 20) enables long-range planning and meaning construction but also enables rumination, regret, and anticipatory anxiety. The capacity for self-modeling enables identity and agency but also enables self-deception, shame, and identity crisis. The capacity for shared representation (Rung 22) enables culture and cooperation but also enables conformity, propaganda, and collective self-deception.

These are not design flaws that better engineering could eliminate. They are structural consequences of the coherence architecture that evolution produced — tradeoffs inherent in any system complex enough to sustain the kind of psychological life that humans live. Understanding them as tradeoffs rather than pathologies is essential for both clinical practice and cultural design.

11.2.3 The Mismatch Problem

Evolutionary psychology has emphasized the concept of mismatch: the idea that psychological mechanisms evolved under ancestral conditions and may be maladaptive in modern environments. CU refines this concept. The mismatch is not merely between evolved mechanisms and modern stimuli — between a sugar-craving brain and a sugar-abundant environment. It is between coherence architectures evolved for one kind of coherence landscape and the radically different coherence landscape that modernity presents.

Human psychology evolved in environments characterized by small group size (Dunbar, 1992), stable social roles, direct feedback between action and consequence, high physical demand, limited information flow, and shared narrative frameworks that organized meaning across the community. Modern environments present the opposite profile: massive social networks, fluid roles, attenuated feedback, sedentary lifestyle, informational deluge, and fragmented or absent shared narratives. The coherence architecture is the same; the landscape it must navigate has been transformed.

This mismatch is not merely a matter of individual discomfort. It is a structural condition that elevates IES across entire populations — a point that Section 11.4 develops in detail.

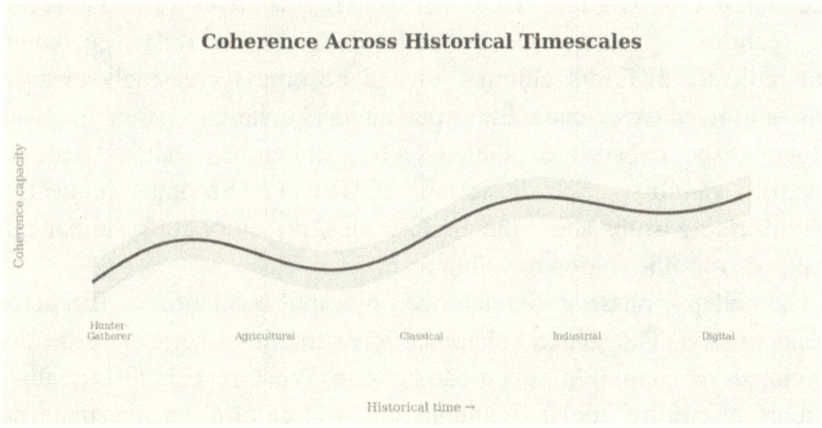

Figure 15. *Civilizational coherence trajectory. Three eras mapped against coherence capacity: pre-modern (high local, low global coherence), modern (expanded scope but fragmented integration), and the present crisis (unprecedented capability with declining coherence infrastructure).*

11.3 Civilizational History

At the level of civilizations, coherence dynamics operate across centuries and millennia. Societies develop institutions, norms, and narratives to maintain coherence across vast numbers of individuals — the Ladder's progression from Rung 24 (Norm Formation) through Rung 26 (Culture). When these structures align with lived experience and material conditions, they support flourishing. When they drift out of alignment, coherence degrades — first slowly, then catastrophically.

11.3.1 The Rise and Fall Pattern

The rise and fall of civilizations follows a recognizable coherence pattern. In the constructive phase, shared coherence fields strengthen: institutions consolidate, narratives stabilize, norms align with material conditions, and individual regulatory burden decreases as collective scaffolding deepens. In the mature phase, the civilization achieves high collective FCS — its members experience meaning, stability, and purpose within well-functioning institutional frameworks.

In the decline phase, one or more of the following coherence failures accumulates: institutions drift from the conditions they were designed to serve, maintaining procedural coherence while losing functional coherence (CU-CL-7, Cultural Time Horizons). Narratives fail to integrate new realities — technological change, demographic shifts, encounters with radically different cultures — and become increasingly distorted relative to lived experience. Elites pursue local coherence (wealth, power, status) at the expense of the collective coherence that sustains the system's viability. Self-deception (CU-Ψ11) becomes collective: uncomfortable truths about the civilization's trajectory are systematically excluded from the shared meaning map.

The collapse phase is characterized by rapid escalation of IES across the population. The shared coherence infrastructure degrades faster than individuals or communities can compensate. What appears historically as political instability, social fragmentation, and cultural decline manifests psychologically as anxiety, depression, meaninglessness, polarization, and the desperate search for alternative coherence sources — religious revival, ideological radicalization, charismatic leadership, substance use. These are coherence-seeking responses to coherence withdrawal, structurally identical to the individual-level compensatory strategies described in Section 7.4.

11.3.2 Periods of Transformation

Not all civilizational disruption is decline. Some periods of intense coherence challenge produce genuine reorganization — the civilizational analogue of the post-traumatic growth described in Section 7.2.2. The Axial Age (approximately 800–200 BCE), which produced the philosophical and religious traditions that still organize much of human meaning — Confucianism, Buddhism, Greek philosophy, Abrahamic monotheism — can be understood as a period of civilizational-scale coherence reorganization, in which old meaning structures had collapsed and new, more abstract, more universalizable coherence frameworks emerged to replace them.

The scientific revolution and the Enlightenment represent another such reorganization: the construction of new coherence frameworks (empiricism, rational inquiry, natural law, individual rights) that could integrate the accumulated evidence that medieval coherence structures could no longer accommodate. These transitions were not smooth. They involved centuries of conflict, confusion, and suffering — the civilizational separatrix-crossing is no less painful than the individual one described in Section 8.6.

11.4 The Present Moment

The present era is characterized by conditions that produce unprecedented coherence challenges — challenges that no prior human society has faced and for which existing coherence architectures are inadequately prepared.

11.4.1 The Mechanisms of Modern IES

Several features of modernity operate as population-level IES generators:

Informational density. The human system evolved to process information at rates orders of magnitude lower than what digital environments now deliver. The result is not merely "information overload" in the folk sense but a chronic elevation of coherence demands: every piece of information is a potential perturbation to the meaning map, and the system must either integrate it (costly) or filter it (requiring active regulatory effort). The sheer volume of information to which modern humans are exposed ensures that integration is impossible and filtering is exhausting.

Social comparison at scale. Social media and digital connectivity expose individuals to vastly expanded comparison sets — hundreds or thousands of curated self-presentations rather than the small group of directly known others that ancestral environments provided. The system's social-coherence mechanisms (Rungs 22–23) were not designed for this scale of input. The result is chronic evaluation anxiety, identity instability, and the relentless sense that one's own life is inadequate relative to the displayed lives of others.

Meaning structure erosion. The shared narrative frameworks that historically organized meaning — religious traditions, cultural identities, stable community roles, intergenerational continuity — have weakened under the combined pressure of secularization, geographic mobility, institutional distrust, and cultural fragmentation. The longest-horizon coherence structures (Rung 21) are degrading without adequate replacement, producing the meaning vacuum that Section 4.6 identifies as the deepest source of motivational collapse.

Algorithmic engagement optimization. Digital platforms are designed to maximize engagement — which, in CU terms, means capturing coherence drive (CU-Ψ5) and directing it toward interactions that produce short-horizon IES reduction (novelty, outrage, validation) while degrading long-horizon coherence (sustained attention, deep relationships, meaning construction). The dopaminergic coherence-gradient sensitizer (Appendix C, §C.2) is recruited into service of platform engagement metrics, producing the characteristic pattern of compulsive use, reduced attention span, and progressive difficulty sustaining the kinds of extended engagement that long-horizon coherence requires.

11.4.2 Degraded Coherence Support

These IES generators operate against a background of degraded coherence support. The social rungs of the Ladder — Rungs 22 through 26 — are simultaneously weakening:

Shared representations (Rung 22) are fragmenting. Populations no longer share a common informational substrate: different communities inhabit different media ecosystems, consume different narratives, and construct different meaning maps of the same reality. The precondition for coordination — shared models of the world — is eroding.

Coordination dynamics (Rung 23) are degrading. Trust in institutions, experts, and fellow citizens has declined across developed democracies (Putnam, 2000; Twenge et al., 2014). The mutual prediction and adjustment that Rung 23 requires cannot operate when agents no longer trust the predictability of other agents' behavior.

Norms (Rung 24) are destabilizing. Rapid cultural change means that behavioral expectations shift faster than individuals can adapt, producing chronic normative uncertainty — the experience of not knowing what the rules are, or whether there are rules at all.

Institutions (Rung 25) are losing legitimacy. From government to media to education to religion, the institutional scaffolding that maintained collective coherence is perceived as untrustworthy, captured, or irrelevant — withdrawing the stabilizing structure on which millions of individual coherence strategies depended.

Culture (Rung 26) is fragmenting into subcultures, echo chambers, and identity groups, each maintaining local coherence while losing the capacity for cross-group integration that civilizational coherence requires.

11.4.3 The Diagnostic Reframing

This analysis explains the paradox that has puzzled public health researchers: the coexistence of extraordinary material prosperity, cognitive capacity, and technological power with widespread psychological distress. Humans have never been more informed, yet rarely more confused about how to live. The problem is not lack of intelligence, lack of information, or lack of resources. It is the overextension of coherence capacity without adequate support — a population-level coherence crisis in which individual psychological systems are asked to compensate for collapsing social and cultural integration.

Understanding psychology through the lens of coherence allows us to situate individual suffering within this broader temporal arc. It reframes distress not as personal failure, or chemical imbalance, or cognitive distortion, but as a signal that coherence demands exceed available resources — a signal that is accurate, adaptive, and informative, even when it is painful. The signal is doing exactly what it should: alerting the system that its current configuration is non-viable under present conditions.

It also clarifies that sustainable psychological health requires not only individual intervention but collective reorganization. Therapy can restore individual coherence. Medication can reduce individual IES. But neither can rebuild the shared coherence infrastructure that collective life requires. That requires institutional reform, community reconstruction, technology design that respects coherence constraints, and cultural innovation that creates new shared meaning structures adequate to present conditions — the four domains of intervention identified in the Introduction (Section 1.5).

With this temporal perspective established — from individual development through evolutionary history to civilizational dynamics and the unprecedented conditions of the present — we are now in a position to make the core explanatory claim explicit. The final section draws together the threads of the paper and articulates why coherence is the best foundational concept for psychology.

This section has placed psychological coherence in temporal context — from individual development through evolutionary timescales to civilizational history. The coherence dynamics identified in earlier sections operate at every timescale, with the modern era representing a distinctive challenge: unprecedented capacity for domain-specific coherence combined with unprecedented fragmentation of cross-domain integration.

Section 12: Why Coherence Is the Best Explanation

This paper has advanced a simple but far-reaching claim: coherence is the most important foundational concept in psychology. This claim is not offered as a definitional stipulation, a theoretical preference, or a bid for conceptual territory. It is offered as an inference to the best explanation — the same inferential form that the broader CU project employs across every domain it addresses.

The argument has been cumulative. Across ten sections, we have examined the core domains of psychology — perception, cognition, memory (Section 3), emotion and motivation (Section 4), identity, personality, and self (Section 5), sexuality, attachment, and intimacy (Section 6), trauma, neurodiversity, and psychopathology (Section 7), therapy and healing practices (Section 8), moral, political, and meaning systems (Section 9), group psychology, culture, and religion (Section 10), and development, evolution, and history (Section 11). In each case, coherence has emerged not as an optional metaphor or organizing theme but as the underlying constraint that determines whether psychological systems function, fragment, or collapse.

The question is whether any competing foundational concept explains as much, across as many domains, with fewer ad hoc assumptions. The answer, this section argues, is no.

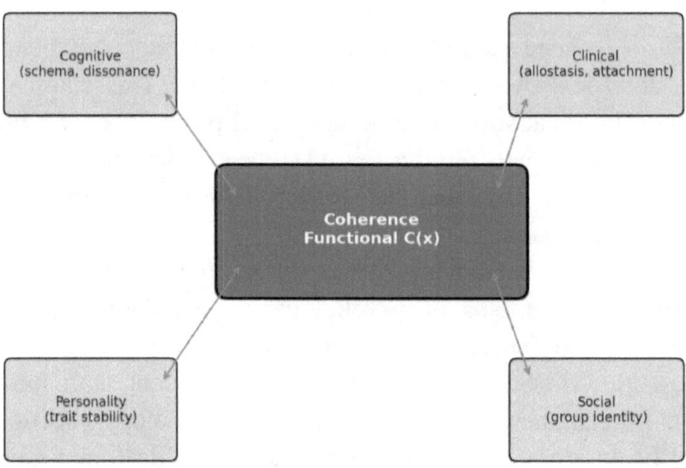

Figure 16. *Coherence as unifying explanatory principle. Comparison of how coherence subsumes constructs from cognitive (schema, dissonance), clinical (allostasis, attachment), personality (trait stability), and social (group identity) psychology under a single formal framework.*

12.1 What Coherence Explains That Other Concepts Do Not

Psychology's existing foundational concepts — representation, reinforcement, adaptation, information processing, narrative, attachment, self-regulation — each illuminate important features of psychological life. Coherence does not replace them. It identifies the structural condition that makes them intelligible as aspects of a single phenomenon rather than as competing partial theories.

Cognitive theories explain how representations are formed, stored, and manipulated. They account for learning, reasoning, and decision-making with considerable precision. But they struggle to explain why certain representations destabilize experience while others support agency, why beliefs that are demonstrably false can be psychologically stabilizing, and why insight alone so often fails to produce change. Coherence explains these puzzles: representations function within a meaning map (CU-Ψ2) that must maintain global integrability (CU-Ψ3), and a representation's psychological effect depends not on its truth value alone but on its relationship to the system's overall coherence landscape — whether it increases or decreases distortion D(u), whether it can be integrated without exceeding regulatory capacity.

Emotional theories explain affective signaling with increasing sophistication — from basic emotion theories (Ekman, 1992) through appraisal theories (Lazarus, 1991) to constructionist accounts (Barrett, 2017). But they typically treat emotion either as subordinate to cognition (emotion follows appraisal) or as a parallel system (emotion and cognition interact). Coherence reveals emotion as something more fundamental: the system's felt registration of its own coherence dynamics (Section 4.1–3.2). Anxiety signals elevated IES without navigable gradient. Depression signals entrapment in a local minimum. Joy signals successful coherence restoration. Shame signals identity-threatening coherence failure in the social dimension. Emotion is not secondary to cognition or parallel to it; it is the system's primary mechanism for monitoring whether coherence is being maintained.

Behavioral theories explain patterns of action, reinforcement, and extinction with empirical rigor. But they cannot explain why certain reinforced behaviors undermine identity, why meaning sustains motivation when reinforcement fails, or why behavioral patterns that produce measurable reward can coexist with deepening suffering. Coherence explains these phenomena through the local—global tension (CU-Ψ6): behaviors that provide short-horizon coherence relief (local reinforcement) can degrade long-horizon coherence (global integration), producing the characteristic pattern in which addiction, compulsion, and avoidance feel locally compelling while becoming globally destructive.

Clinical frameworks — the DSM, ICD, and RDoC systems — explain symptom patterns, diagnostic categories, and treatment indications. But they lack a unifying account of why disparate symptoms cluster together, why symptoms shift and migrate across diagnostic categories, why comorbidity is the rule rather than the exception, and why structurally similar interventions work across nominally different disorders. Coherence provides the missing account: symptoms cluster because coherence collapse affects multiple domains simultaneously (CU-Ψ7). Symptoms shift because deep D(u) produces a family of surface configurations. Comorbidity reflects the structural reality that a system whose coherence has failed in one domain rarely maintains coherence in others. The common factors in therapy work (Section 8.1) because they address the structural preconditions for coherence repair — preconditions that are disorder-independent.

Attachment theories explain relational dynamics with considerable depth. But they do not explain why attachment security facilitates cognitive development, why attachment disruption produces somatic symptoms, or why attachment patterns recapitulate across generations. Coherence explains these connections: attachment provides distributed coherence regulation (Section 6.1), and the quality of attachment determines whether the system's viability region V is expanded or contracted — affecting every dimension of functioning that depends on V being large enough to permit exploration, integration, and growth.

In each case, coherence does not contradict the existing theory. It absorbs it — revealing the partial theory as a description of one dimension of a system-level constraint that the partial theory was always tracking without naming.

12.2 The Explanatory Virtues

The coherence framework possesses four explanatory virtues that are individually significant and collectively rare in psychological theory.

First, it explains failure as well as success. Many psychological theories are optimized to model functioning systems. They explain learning, adaptation, performance, and growth. Coherence explains breakdown — why intelligence, insight, or motivation can coexist with suffering, dysfunction, and self-undermining behavior. It explains why local solutions so often produce global problems (CU-Ψ6), why short-term relief can lead to long-term disintegration (Section 4.5), and why the same mechanisms that enable creativity and moral concern also produce vulnerability and susceptibility to collapse (Section 11.2.2). The capacity to explain failure as precisely as success is a hallmark of genuine foundational concepts.

Second, it scales without changing vocabulary. Coherence applies to neural integration (Appendix C), perceptual processing (Section 3.1), emotional regulation (Section 4), personal identity (Section 5), relational dynamics (Section 6), cultural meaning systems (Section 10.3), and civilizational history (Section 11.3) — without requiring a change in explanatory vocabulary at each level. The same concepts — coherence drive (CU-Ψ5), distortion D(u), viability region V, local—global tension (CU-Ψ6), attractor dynamics — operate across all scales. This scale continuity is rare in psychology, where concepts routinely lose coherence themselves when extended beyond their original domain. The fact that "coherence" retains its explanatory power from the neuronal to the civilizational is not a sign of vagueness; it is a sign of structural depth.

Third, it avoids two common failures. It does not collapse psychology into biology or computation (the reductive failure), nor does it retreat into irreducible subjectivity (the romantic failure). It respects the reality of subjective experience — valence is ineliminable (CU-C3), meaning is structurally real (CU-Ψ1), self-deception is not merely a cognitive error but a meaning-map distortion (CU-Ψ11) — while situating experience within a structurally intelligible framework that admits of formal articulation. It achieves what the Consciousness paper calls the "middle path": taking consciousness seriously without mystifying it, and taking structure seriously without eliminating experience.

Fourth, it is normatively constrained without being normatively overreaching. Coherence does not dictate what individuals should value or believe. It specifies what any viable psychological system must respect in order to remain agentive, intelligible, and capable of sustained action. The distinction between pathology and divergence (CU-Ψ7, CU-Ψ8) is grounded in viability, not conformity. The critique of self-deception (CU-Ψ11) is grounded in the structural costs of meaning-map distortion, not in a particular moral framework. The analysis of therapy (CU-Ψ9) is grounded in the system's own coherence drive (CU-Ψ5), not in the therapist's values. This makes the framework applicable across cultural, ideological, and normative contexts without imposing a single vision of the good life — while still providing principled grounds for distinguishing configurations that sustain agency from configurations that destroy it.

12.3 Why Psychological Disagreement Persists

The coherence framework also explains a meta-level puzzle: why psychological theories have competed so vigorously for so long without resolution.

Competing theories frequently capture different aspects of coherence — representation (cognitive theories), affect (emotion theories), narrative (psychodynamic theories), behavior (learning theories), relationship (attachment theories) — without recognizing the system-level constraint that unifies them. Each theory identifies a genuine dimension of coherence and mistakes it for the whole. The result is a field in which every school can marshal impressive evidence for its claims while failing to integrate with schools that have identified different but equally genuine dimensions of the same underlying phenomenon.

Once coherence is made explicit, these theories appear less as rivals and more as partial views of a shared underlying structure. The debate between cognitive and emotional primacy dissolves: both are aspects of coherence maintenance operating at different levels. The tension between individual and social psychology dissolves: both are aspects of coherence operating at different scales. The competition between therapeutic schools dissolves: all effective therapies modulate coherence, targeting different layers (Section 8.2). The fragmentation of the field becomes intelligible not as theoretical immaturity but as the predictable consequence of a foundational concept that was always operative but never named.

12.4 Practical Consequences

Coherence is not merely a theoretical improvement. It has practical consequences that no competing foundational concept generates.

It reframes psychological suffering as a signal of excessive regulatory load or failed integration (CU-Ψ4) rather than as mere deficit, disorder, or chemical imbalance. This reframing is not cosmetic. It changes what clinicians look for (where has coherence failed?), what they aim for (what would support reintegration?), and how they evaluate outcomes (has integrative capacity been restored or merely have symptoms been suppressed?).

It explains why effective therapy works across schools (Section 8.1) — because the common factors are coherence factors — and why certain interventions backfire (Section 8.6) — because premature stabilization prevents the separatrix-crossing that genuine reorganization requires.

It provides a principled basis for distinguishing between difference and dysfunction (CU-Ψ7, CU-Ψ8) — not through statistical norms or social convention but through the structural criterion of viability. A system is pathological when it cannot maintain viable coherence; a system is divergent when it achieves viable coherence through alternative strategies.

It explains why individual treatment cannot fully compensate for collapsing social coherence (Section 10.7, Section 11.4) — because individual coherence depends on distributed regulatory support that therapy alone cannot provide.

And it provides the conceptual bridge to the ethical questions that psychology has always implicitly raised but rarely addressed systematically: if coherence is what makes psychological functioning possible, then practices, institutions, and technologies that systematically degrade coherence are not merely inconvenient — they are destructive of the very capacities that agency, morality, and meaning require.

12.5 The Claim

Taken together, these considerations support the central conclusion of this paper: coherence is the best available unifying explanatory concept for psychology. It explains more, with fewer ad hoc assumptions, across a wider range of phenomena, at more scales of analysis, than competing foundational concepts. It preserves empirical rigor while restoring conceptual unity to a field that has long lacked it. And it generates practical consequences — clinical, institutional, technological — that no purely theoretical advance could produce.

This claim is defeasible. It is offered as an inference to the best explanation, not as a necessary truth. If a competing concept can be shown to explain the same range of phenomena with equal parsimony and greater precision, the claim should be revised. The strength of the claim lies not in dogmatic assertion but in the cumulative weight of the evidence assembled across the preceding sections — evidence that converges, from every direction, on the same structural conclusion.

Section 13: Transitions Forward

The argument of this paper has been that psychology, at its foundation, is the study of how minds maintain coherence over time. Perception, emotion, cognition, identity, attachment, pathology, therapy, morality, group dynamics, development, and history are not isolated domains but interlocking mechanisms that either support or undermine integrated self-regulation (CU-C4, self-affecting dynamics). Making coherence explicit allows these domains to be understood as parts of a single explanatory framework rather than as competing schools or fragmented literatures.

Within the broader Coherence Universalism project, this psychological foundation performs a critical role. It supplies the conceptual bridge between structural accounts of consciousness — the forcing conditions, the coherence functional, the identity conditions — and normative accounts of ethics. Without a clear understanding of how coherence operates within psychological systems — how meaning maps are constructed and distorted, how coherence drive organizes behavior, how self-deception functions and fails, how shared coherence fields sustain and constrain — discussions of agency, responsibility, alignment, and moral failure remain abstract or incomplete.

13.1 The Bridge to Ethics

The implications extend directly into ethics. If psychological coherence is a prerequisite for agency, then moral evaluation must attend to the conditions that preserve or destroy it. This paper has established several results that CU — Ethics takes as foundational:

That self-deception (CU-Ψ11) is not merely a psychological phenomenon but a structural precondition for moral failure — because moral failure requires meaning-map distortion that allows the agent to act against coherence while maintaining the appearance of integrity (Section 4.5, Section 9.5).

That moral reasoning capacity depends on attractor structure (Appendix F) — that systems regulated by social approval reason differently from systems regulated by epistemic coherence, and that moral development consists in the progressive internalization and integration of coherence attractors, not merely the acquisition of moral knowledge.

That moral beliefs function as coherence constraints (Section 9.2) — that morality is not merely a set of abstract principles but a psychological technology for preserving coherence across agents and time, and that the viability of a moral system depends on whether it can sustain coherence without progressive self-deception.

That practices, institutions, and technologies that systematically erode coherence undermine the very capacities that ethical agency presupposes — a result that generates specific obligations regarding institutional design, technology regulation, and the protection of shared coherence fields.

These results supply the psychological content that CU — Ethics formalizes into an ethical framework. Without them, the ethical framework would be structurally sound but empirically empty — specifying what moral agents must be without showing what they are.

13.2 The Bridge to AI

The framework reframes contemporary concerns about artificial intelligence in ways that CU — AI develops at length. Alignment cannot be reduced to optimizing outputs, enforcing rules, or ensuring that AI systems produce correct answers. It must be understood in relation to the psychological coherence of the human systems — individual and collective — with which AI interacts.

Systems that degrade human coherence — even while improving efficiency, accuracy, or productivity — pose a fundamental risk. The mechanisms of modern IES generation identified in Section 11.4 — informational density, social comparison at scale, meaning structure erosion, algorithmic engagement optimization — are substantially mediated or amplified by AI-driven systems. Understanding these mechanisms as coherence dynamics rather than merely as "harms" or "risks" transforms the alignment problem from a technical specification challenge into a structural design challenge: AI systems must be designed to preserve and support human coherence, not merely to avoid explicitly harmful outputs.

13.3 The Bridge to Society

At the societal level, the psychology of coherence clarifies why modern crises of meaning, polarization, and mental health are inseparable (Section 11.4). Individual distress reflects not only personal vulnerability but the breakdown of shared coherence fields (Section 9.7). Sustainable psychological well-being therefore requires attention not only to individual intervention but to the four domains of collective reorganization: institutional reform that restores the legitimacy and function of Rung 25 structures, community reconstruction that rebuilds the distributed regulatory infrastructure that individual coherence depends on, technology design that respects coherence constraints rather than exploiting coherence drive for engagement metrics, and cultural innovation that creates shared meaning structures adequate to the conditions of the present.

13.4 What This Paper Has Not Done

This paper has not attempted to resolve every question in psychology. Its aim has been more modest and more demanding: to identify the structural constraint that psychology has always been navigating, often implicitly, and to show why making that constraint explicit matters.

It has not provided complete formal models of every phenomenon it discusses. The formal apparatus — meaning space M, meaning maps Φ, Field Coherence Score, Inverse Entropic Stress, distortion D(u), viability region V — is articulated in Appendix B and employed throughout the paper at the level of structural precision rather than quantitative prediction. The development of fully quantitative models remains future work, to be pursued in collaboration with the empirical research programs that this framework is intended to inform and organize.

It has not resolved the relationship between coherence and truth. The paper has argued that coherence is the most important foundational concept in psychology — that it explains psychological functioning and failure better than any competing concept. It has not argued that coherence is all there is, or that truth reduces to coherence, or that anything goes so long as it feels coherent. The viability criterion (Section 9.6) constrains which coherence configurations are sustainable, and CU's broader commitment to the reality of moral structure (Introduction, Section 1.3) ensures that coherence is not reduced to mere self-consistency. But the full articulation of how coherence and truth relate — how discovered moral structure constrains viable coherence without being reducible to it — belongs to the ethical and metaphysical papers rather than the psychological one.

13.5 Closing

Coherence is not a panacea. It does not eliminate conflict, difference, or uncertainty. It specifies the conditions under which conflict can be integrated rather than destructive, difference can be accommodated rather than pathologized, and uncertainty can be navigated without collapse.

Psychology's task, seen in this light, is not to produce perfectly optimized minds but to support viable ones — minds capable of integrating experience, sustaining agency, and acting meaningfully over time. Coherence Universalism offers a framework for understanding and pursuing that task with greater clarity, greater precision, and deeper connection to the structural conditions that make psychological life possible.

The twelve principles defined in this paper — from CU-Ψ1 (Meaning Space) through CU-Ψ12 (Shared Coherence Fields) — are not the last word on the psychology of coherence. They are the first systematic articulation of what psychology has always been about, made explicit so that it can be examined, tested, refined, and extended. The work continues in CU — Ethics, CU — AI, and in every clinical encounter, every institutional design, and every cultural innovation that takes the coherence of human minds seriously enough to protect it.

References

Ainsworth, M. D. S., Blehar, M. C., Waters, E., & Wall, S. (1978). *Patterns of attachment: A psychological study of the strange

Rader, G. K. D. (2026a). Coherence Universalism — Metaphysics and Epistemology: Coherence Logic and an Introduction to the Coherence Ladder. Heaven≡Earth Press.

Rader, G. K. D. (2026b). Coherence Universalism — Foundations: The Principle Architecture. Heaven≡Earth Press.

Rader, G. K. D. (2026c). Coherence Universalism — Physics: Coherence Dynamics, Emergent Spacetime, and the Laws of Physical Order. Heaven≡Earth Press.

Rader, G. K. D. (2026d). Coherence Universalism — Biology: Coherence as the Organizing Principle of Living Systems. Heaven≡Earth Press.

Rader, G. K. D. (2026e). Coherence Universalism — Psychology: Coherence as the Structural Foundation of Mind, Meaning, and Mental Health. Heaven≡Earth Press.

Rader, G. K. D. (2026f). Coherence Universalism — Consciousness: Why Experience Is Constituted by Coherence Under Constraint. Heaven≡Earth Press.

Rader, G. K. D. (2026g). Coherence Universalism — Ethics: Values, Normative Orientation, and Justificatory Integrity. Heaven≡Earth Press.

Rader, G. K. D. (2026h). Coherence Universalism — Social Dynamics: Coherence Strategies, Institutional Design, and the Present Crisis. Heaven≡Earth Press.

Rader, G. K. D. (2026i). Coherence Universalism — Artificial Intelligence: Consciousness, Alignment, and the Future of Intelligence. Heaven≡Earth Press.

situation*. Lawrence Erlbaum Associates.

Asch, S. E. (1951). Effects of group pressure upon the modification and distortion of judgments. In H. Guetzkow (Ed.), *Groups, leadership, and men* (pp. 177–190). Carnegie Press.

Barrett, L. F. (2017). *How emotions are made: The secret life of the brain*. Houghton Mifflin Harcourt.

Bartlett, F. C. (1932). *Remembering: A study in experimental and social psychology*. Cambridge University Press.

Baumeister, R. F., & Leary, M. R. (1995). The need to belong: Desire for interpersonal attachments as a fundamental human motivation. *Psychological Bulletin, 117*(3), 497–529.

Beck, A. T. (1976). *Cognitive therapy and the emotional disorders.* International Universities Press.

Blumenthal, J. A., Babyak, M. A., Doraiswamy, P. M., Watkins, L., Hoffman, B. M., Barbour, K. A., Herman, S., Craighead, W. E., Brosse, A. L., Waugh, R., Hinderliter, A., & Sherwood, A. (2007). Exercise and pharmacotherapy in the treatment of major depressive disorder. *Psychosomatic Medicine, 69*(7), 587–596.

Bowen, M. (1978). *Family therapy in clinical practice.* Jason Aronson.

Bowlby, J. (1969). *Attachment and loss: Vol. 1. Attachment.* Basic Books.

Bruner, J. (1990). *Acts of meaning.* Harvard University Press.

Cacioppo, J. T., & Hawkley, L. C. (2009). Perceived social isolation and cognition. *Trends in Cognitive Sciences, 13*(10), 447–454.

Carhart-Harris, R. L., & Friston, K. J. (2019). REBUS and the anarchic brain: Toward a unified model of the brain action of psychedelics. *Pharmacological Reviews, 71*(3), 316–344.

Carhart-Harris, R. L., Leech, R., Hellyer, P. J., Shanahan, M., Feilding, A., Tagliazucchi, E., Chialvo, D. R., & Nutt, D. (2014). The entropic brain: A theory of conscious states informed by neuroimaging research with psychedelic drugs. *Frontiers in Human Neuroscience, 8*,

Case, A., & Deaton, A. (2015). Rising morbidity and mortality in midlife among white non-Hispanic Americans in the 21st century. *Proceedings of the National Academy of Sciences, 112*(49), 15078–15083.

Case, A., & Deaton, A. (2020). *Deaths of despair and the future of capitalism.* Princeton University Press.

Clark, A. (2013). Whatever next? Predictive brains, situated agents, and the future of cognitive science. *Behavioral and Brain Sciences, 36*(3), 181–204.

Cooley, C. H. (1902). *Human nature and the social order.* Charles Scribner's Sons.

Costa, P. T., Jr., & McCrae, R. R. (1992). *Revised NEO Personality Inventory (NEO PI-R) and NEO Five-Factor Inventory (NEO-FFI) professional manual.* Psychological Assessment Resources.

Damasio, A. R. (1994). *Descartes' error: Emotion, reason, and the human brain*. G. P. Putnam's Sons.

Damasio, A. R. (1999). *The feeling of what happens: Body and emotion in the making of consciousness*. Harcourt Brace.

Deci, E. L., & Ryan, R. M. (2000). The "what" and "why" of goal pursuits: Human needs and the self-determination of behavior. *Psychological Inquiry, 11*(4), 227–268.

Dunbar, R. I. M. (1992). Neocortex size as a constraint on group size in primates. *Journal of Human Evolution, 22*(6), 469–493.

Durkheim, É. (1897/1951). *Suicide: A study in sociology* (J. A. Spaulding & G. Simpson, Trans.). Free Press. (Original work published 1897)

Durkheim, É. (1912/1995). *The elementary forms of religious life* (K. E. Fields, Trans.). Free Press. (Original work published 1912)

Ekman, P. (1992). An argument for basic emotions. *Cognition and Emotion, 6*(3–4), 169–200.

Ellis, A. (1962). *Reason and emotion in psychotherapy*. Lyle Stuart.

Erikson, E. H. (1968). *Identity: Youth and crisis*. W. W. Norton.

Festinger, L. (1957). *A theory of cognitive dissonance*. Stanford University Press.

Frankl, V. E. (1946/2006). *Man's search for meaning* (I. Lasch, Trans.). Beacon Press. (Original work published 1946)

Freud, S. (1917/1957). Mourning and melancholia. In J. Strachey (Ed. & Trans.), *The standard edition of the complete psychological works of Sigmund Freud* (Vol. 14, pp. 237–258). Hogarth Press. (Original work published 1917)

Friston, K. (2010). The free-energy principle: A unified brain theory? *Nature Reviews Neuroscience, 11*(2), 127–138.

Greene, J. D. (2013). *Moral tribes: Emotion, reason, and the gap between us and them*. Penguin Press.

Gross, J. J. (2002). Emotion regulation: Affective, cognitive, and social consequences. *Psychophysiology, 39*(3), 281–291.

Haidt, J. (2001). The emotional dog and its rational tail: A social intuitionist approach to moral judgment. *Psychological Review, 108*(4), 814–834.

Haidt, J. (2012). *The righteous mind: Why good people are divided by politics and religion*. Vintage Books.

Hazan, C., & Shaver, P. (1987). Romantic love conceptualized as an attachment process. *Journal of Personality and Social Psychology*, *52*(3), 511–524.

Herman, J. L. (1992). *Trauma and recovery: The aftermath of violence — from domestic abuse to political terror*. Basic Books.

Hofer, M. A. (1994). Hidden regulators in attachment, separation, and loss. *Monographs of the Society for Research in Child Development*, *59*(2–3), 192–207.

Hohwy, J. (2013). *The predictive mind*. Oxford University Press.

Holt-Lunstad, J., Smith, T. B., & Layton, J. B. (2010). Social relationships and mortality risk: A meta-analytic review. *PLoS Medicine*, *7*(7), e1000316.

Hull, C. L. (1943). *Principles of behavior: An introduction to behavior theory*. Appleton-Century-Crofts.

Janis, I. L. (1972). *Victims of groupthink: A psychological study of foreign-policy decisions and fiascoes*. Houghton Mifflin.

Janoff-Bulman, R. (1992). *Shattered assumptions: Towards a new psychology of trauma*. Free Press.

Kahneman, D. (2011). *Thinking, fast and slow*. Farrar, Straus and Giroux.

Kahneman, D., & Tversky, A. (1974). Judgment under uncertainty: Heuristics and biases. *Science*, *185*(4157), 1124–1131.

Kegan, R. (1982). *The evolving self: Problem and process in human development*. Harvard University Press.

Kohlberg, L. (1981). *Essays on moral development: Vol. 1. The philosophy of moral development*. Harper & Row.

Lazarus, R. S. (1991). *Emotion and adaptation*. Oxford University Le Bon, G. (1895/2002). *The crowd: A study of the popular mind*. Dover Publications. (Original work published 1895)

Levine, P. A. (1997). *Waking the tiger: Healing trauma*. North Atlantic Books.

Loftus, E. F. (2005). Planting misinformation in the human mind: A 30-year investigation of the malleability of memory. *Learning& Memory*, *12*(4), 361–366.

Luborsky, L., Singer, B., & Luborsky, L. (1975). Comparative studies of psychotherapies: Is it true that "everyone has won and all must have prizes"? *Archives of General Psychiatry*, *32*(8), 995–1008.

Main, M., & Hesse, E. (1990). Parents' unresolved traumatic experiences are related to infant disorganized attachment status: Is frightened and/or frightening parental behavior the linking mechanism? In M. T. Greenberg, D. Cicchetti, & E. M. Cummings (Eds.), *Attachment in the preschool years: Theory, research, and intervention* (pp. 161–182). University of Chicago Press.

McAdams, D. P. (2001). The psychology of life stories. *Review of General Psychology*, *5*(2), 100–122.

Mead, G. H. (1934). *Mind, self, and society from the standpoint of a social behaviorist* (C. W. Morris, Ed.). University of Chicago Press.

Milgram, S. (1963). Behavioral study of obedience. *Journal of Abnormal and Social Psychology*, *67*(4), 371–378.

Minuchin, S. (1974). *Families and family therapy*. Harvard University

Mischel, W. (1968). *Personality and assessment*. Wiley.

Mitchell, S. A., & Black, M. J. (1995). *Freud and beyond: A history of modern psychoanalytic thought*. Basic Books.

Ogden, P., Minton, K., & Pain, C. (2006). *Trauma and the body: A sensorimotor approach to psychotherapy*. W. W. Norton.

Piaget, J. (1954). *The construction of reality in the child* (M. Cook, Trans.). Basic Books.

Putnam, R. D. (2000). *Bowling alone: The collapse and revival of American community*. Simon & Schuster.

Rosenzweig, S. (1936). Some implicit common factors in diverse methods of psychotherapy. *American Journal of Orthopsychiatry*, *6*(3), 412–415.

Sbarra, D. A., & Hazan, C. (2008). Coregulation, dysregulation, self-regulation: An integrative analysis and empirical agenda for understanding adult attachment, separation, loss, and recovery. *Personality and Social Psychology Review*, *12*(2), 141–167.

Schacter, D. L. (1996). *Searching for memory: The brain, the mind, and the past*. Basic Books.

Schuch, F. B., Vancampfort, D., Richards, J., Rosenbaum, S., Ward, P. B., & Stubbs, B. (2016). Exercise as a treatment for depression: A meta-analysis adjusting for publication bias. *Journal of Psychiatric Research*, *77*, 42–51.

Twenge, J. M., Campbell, W. K., & Carter, N. T. (2014). Declines in trust in others and confidence in institutions among American adults and late adolescents, 1972–2012. *Psychological Science*, *25*(10), 1914–1923.

van der Kolk, B. A. (2014). *The body keeps the score: Brain, mind, and body in the healing of trauma*. Viking.

Vygotsky, L. S. (1978). *Mind in society: The development of higher psychological processes* (M. Cole, V. John-Steiner, S. Scribner, & E. Souberman, Eds.). Harvard University Press.

Wampold, B. E. (2001). *The great psychotherapy debate: Models, methods, and findings*. Lawrence Erlbaum Associates.

Wampold, B. E. (2015). How important are the common factors in psychotherapy? An update. *World Psychiatry*, *14*(3), 270–277.

White, M., & Epston, D. (1990). *Narrative means to therapeutic ends*. W. W. Norton.

Glossary of Psychology-Specific Terms

This glossary defines the key terms and formal constructs used throughout the paper, organized alphabetically. Principle codes (e.g., CU-Ψ1) are given where applicable to facilitate cross-referencing with the formal apparatus.

Attractor. A state or region in a dynamical system toward which the system tends to evolve, especially under perturbation. In CU psychology, attractors correspond to the regulatory patterns that dominate under stress — what the system "falls back on" when coherence is threatened. See Appendix F for the developmental attractor profiles.

Attractor basin. The region of state space from which trajectories converge to a given attractor. A deep basin means the system strongly resists perturbation away from that attractor; a shallow basin means the system is more easily displaced. Therapeutic change often requires crossing the boundary (separatrix) between attractor basins (Section 7.6).

Coherence. The integrated, constraint-satisfying organization of a system across its relevant domains and timescales. Coherence is graded (CU-FP2), multi-scale (CU-FP4), and constrained (CU-FP3). It is not synonymous with consistency, rigidity, or internal agreement; it denotes the structural condition that makes psychological functioning possible.

Coherence collapse. The failure of a system to maintain viable coherence — the point at which the system's configuration exits the viability region V. Manifests psychologically as decompensation, psychotic break, dissociative crisis, or identity dissolution. See CU-Ψ7.

Coherence drive (CU-Ψ5). The constitutive motivation of psychological systems to reduce incoherence. Not a preference or learned behavior but a structural feature of any system that must maintain integrated regulation to remain viable. Operates continuously, automatically, and often unconsciously.

Coherence functional C(u). The system-level measure of coherence defined in the Consciousness paper. For a given configuration u in state space H, C(u) quantifies the degree of integrated, constraint-satisfying organization. In psychology, C(u) is translated as the Field Coherence Score (FCS). See Appendix B, §B.8.

Coherence gradient ∇C(u). The direction in state space along which coherence increases most steeply. Psychological systems navigate coherence landscapes via gradients rather than absolute optima (CU-D4). Valence is the felt aspect of this gradient.

Coherence landscape. The topography of the coherence functional across state space — the pattern of peaks (coherence optima), valleys (local minima), ridges, and saddle points that determines which configurations are stable, which are accessible, and which transitions are possible.

Compensatory strategy. A regulatory response that reduces felt IES without resolving the underlying coherence challenge. Examples include emotional suppression, rigid belief formation, avoidance, dissociation, self-deception, and substance use. Compensatory strategies preserve short-term viability at long-term coherence cost (Section 7.4).

D(u) — Distortion. The deviation between a system's current configuration and its nearest coherence maximum. High D(u) means the system is far from optimal coherence; low D(u) means the system is close to a coherence optimum. IES is the felt registration of elevated D(u).

FCS — Field Coherence Score (CU-Ψ3). A system-level measure of how well an agent's meaning map supports integrated regulation across domains and time. FCS ∝ Integrability / Regulatory Load. High FCS = stable, flexible, meaningful functioning. Low FCS = fragmentation, brittleness, exhaustion. See Appendix B, §B.3.

IES — Inverse Entropic Stress (CU-Ψ4). The felt and functional pressure on a system when coherence demands exceed regulatory capacity. IES ∝ Coherence Demands − Regulatory Capacity. Chronic elevation of IES produces compensatory strategies and, if sustained, coherence collapse. See Appendix B, §B.4.

Identity conditions (CU-I1 through CU-I5). The five conditions that must be satisfied for a system to have genuine identity: viability constraints (CU-I1), constraint persistence across substrate change (CU-I2), irreversible path-dependence (CU-I3), self-referential constraint enforcement (CU-I4), and identity collapse thresholds (CU-I5). See Supplementary Appendix II.

Local—global tension (CU-Ψ6). The structural principle that coherence optimized within a single domain or timescale may degrade coherence across domains or timescales. The single most important structural principle in CU psychology. Explains why locally rational strategies produce globally irrational outcomes.

M — Meaning space (CU-Ψ1). The structured landscape in which an agent evaluates experiences, beliefs, values, identities, and possible actions. A high-dimensional state space whose dimensions correspond to psychologically relevant variables. See Appendix B, §B.1.

Meaning map — Φ (CU-Ψ2). The agent's internal representation of meaning space: a compressed, approximate model that allows navigation without exhaustive computation. $\Phi : \text{Experience} \rightarrow M$. Meaning maps are necessarily lossy compressions that trade accuracy for navigability. See Appendix B, §B.2.

Neurodiversity (CU-Ψ8). Alternative coherence strategies that achieve viability through non-dominant pathways. Divergent architectures are distinguished from pathology by their capacity for viable coherence, not by their conformity to statistical norms. See Section 7.3.

Psychopathology (CU-Ψ7). Persistent failure to maintain viable coherence — the system cannot sustain integrated regulation under its current constraints. Distinguished from divergence by the viability criterion: a system is pathological when it cannot maintain viable coherence, not when it deviates from norms.

Self-deception (CU-Ψ11). Meaning-map distortion that preserves local coherence at the expense of global integrability. The distorted map Φ' avoids regions of M that threaten identity coherence. Reduces felt IES in the short term but increases cumulative D(u) over time. See Appendix B, §B.6.

Separatrix. The boundary between attractor basins in a dynamical system. Crossing a separatrix requires temporary destabilization — the system must leave one basin of stability before reaching another. In therapy, this corresponds to the period of increased distress that genuine reorganization sometimes requires (Section 8.6).

Shared coherence field (CU-Ψ12). A distributed regulatory structure in which multiple agents' coherence is jointly maintained through coordinated representations, norms, practices, and narrative. Individual coherence within the field depends partly on the field's stability; the field's stability depends partly on individual participation. See Section 9.

Therapy as coherence modulation (CU-Ψ9). Therapeutic intervention restores psychological viability by modulating the system's position within its coherence landscape — reducing D(u), lowering IES, increasing FCS, or enabling transition to a more globally coherent attractor basin. See Section 7.

V — Viability region. The region of state space within which the system's identity conditions remain satisfied — the set of configurations the system must not leave if it is to persist as this system. The boundary of V defines the collapse thresholds beyond which recovery is impossible. See CU-I5.

Valence. The felt quality of coherence dynamics — the system's experiential registration of whether coherence is increasing (positive valence) or decreasing (negative valence). Valence is ineliminable from conscious experience (CU-C3) and constitutes the primary mechanism through which the system monitors its own coherence.

Supplementary Appendix H — The Coherence Ladder: Rungs Referenced in This Paper

The Coherence Ladder is the central organizational structure of Coherence Universalism, tracing the emergence of increasingly complex coherence from pure structure through consciousness to normative reasoning. This paper draws primarily on Rungs 11–30. The complete Ladder (Rungs 1–33) is presented in *Coherence Universalism: The Transcendental Framework*. Below are the rungs referenced in this paper, with the text paraphrased from the Framework document.

Rungs 11–15: From Physics to Life

Rung 11: Far-from-Equilibrium Structure. Coherence that persists by actively exporting entropy rather than passively decaying. Unlike equilibrium structures, far-from-equilibrium structures require continuous throughput of energy and matter to maintain organization. This establishes the physical precondition for life but does not yet constitute life itself.

Rung 12: Metabolic Coherence. Internal processes actively reorganize matter and energy to sustain structural organization. The system no longer merely benefits from favorable flows; it harnesses and regulates them. This marks the transition from passive persistence to active regulation.

Rung 13: Self-Maintenance. Coherence constrains dynamics by requiring its own continued existence as a condition on admissible change. The system's organization becomes a governing constraint on its behavior: processes that undermine coherence are suppressed, while those that preserve it are favored. This reflexive condition distinguishes living systems from merely complex physical processes.

Rung 14: Adaptive Constraint Satisfaction. A self-maintaining system modifies its own constraints in response to environmental pressure. Rather than relying on fixed regulatory mechanisms, the system alters how it preserves coherence when circumstances change. This introduces plasticity and learning at the biological level.

Rung 15: Life. Coherence that actively resists its own dissipation through self-maintenance and adaptive constraint satisfaction. Life is not defined by particular substances or molecular mechanisms but by this functional organization: a living system is one for which continued coherence is the central organizing principle of dynamics.

Rungs 16–21: From Representation to Meaning

Rung 16: Internal Models. A living system maintains compressed representations of itself and its environment. These representations allow the system to distinguish internal from external states and to anticipate how changes will affect coherence. Internal models do not require consciousness; they require only that the system encode structured regularities relevant to its persistence.

Rung 17: Predictive Coherence. Coherence is evaluated relative to anticipated future states rather than only present stability. The system uses its internal models to project forward and assess which actions are likely to preserve coherence over time. This introduces a temporal horizon into coherence evaluation.

Rung 18: Error Correction. Discrepancies between predicted and actual outcomes drive updates to internal models. These prediction errors become signals that guide learning and adaptation. Error correction allows coherence to be preserved through continual revision rather than rigid control.

Rung 19: Agency. A system selects actions specifically to preserve coherence across anticipated futures. Actions are no longer mere responses to stimuli; they are interventions chosen because of their predicted effects on coherence. Agency is a structural property of predictive systems, not an all-or-nothing metaphysical status.

Rung 20: Subjective Time. Predictive coherence integrates memory of past states with anticipation of future ones into a unified internal narrative. Time becomes an internally experienced structure organizing perception and action, not merely an external ordering of events.

Rung 21: Meaning. Elements of experience are evaluated in terms of their relevance to coherence preservation. A signal, object, or event is meaningful insofar as it informs the system about how to act to preserve coherence across futures. Meaning is relational, context-sensitive, and grounded in the functional role of representations within a predictive system.

Rungs 22–26: Social and Cultural Coherence

Rung 22: Shared Representations. Coherence is distributed across agents through language, symbols, and practices. These representations allow multiple systems to coordinate by aligning internal models. Coherence is no longer confined to individual agents; it spans social networks.

Rung 23: Coordination Dynamics. Agents adjust behavior to maintain shared coherence. Social order arises from mutual prediction, feedback, and alignment — not from external imposition. Successful coordination stabilizes shared representations; failed coordination leads to fragmentation.

Rung 24: Norm Formation. Certain coordination patterns stabilize and become expected. Norms function as attractors in social coherence space, guiding behavior without constant negotiation. They reduce uncertainty and cognitive load by constraining possible actions.

Rung 25: Institutions. Norms are formalized and enforced across time and scale. Institutions encode constraints that stabilize social coherence beyond individual lifespans. They reduce volatility but also introduce rigidity, creating tradeoffs between stability and adaptability.

Rung 26: Culture. High-level coherence that persists across generations through shared narratives, practices, and values. Culture integrates norms, institutions, and representations into relatively stable patterns. It is the memory of social systems.

Rungs 27–30: Normative Coherence

Rung 27: Value Differentiation. Some coherence patterns are recognized as promoting flourishing while others undermine it. Not all stable coherence is desirable; some forms systematically destroy coherence elsewhere or in the future. Differentiating value requires evaluating coherence across agents and timescales.

Rung 28: Harm Detection. Harm is identified as the destruction or degradation of coherence across agents or time. Harm detection requires recognizing negative externalities and delayed effects. This expands coherence evaluation beyond local optimization.

Rung 29: Tradeoff Resolution. Coherence demands often conflict. Preserving coherence in one domain may reduce it in another. Ethical reasoning manages these conflicts by balancing competing constraints. The question is not whether to make tradeoffs but how to make them well.

Rung 30: Norm Justification. Ethical constraints must be defended with reasons that generalize beyond immediate interests. Justification enables trust, coordination, and legitimacy. Without justification, norms cannot scale or persist.

Supplementary Appendix II — Foundational Principles Referenced in This Paper

This paper draws on principles defined across several documents in the Coherence Universalism project. This appendix collects the definitions of all non-psychology-specific principles cited in the main text and appendices, organized by category. The full development of each principle appears in its originating document; these summaries provide the minimum context needed for this paper's arguments.

II.1 Foundational Principles (CU-FP)

CU-FP1. Coherence as Transcendental Condition. Wherever persistence, structure, meaning, agency, or normativity appear, coherence is a necessary condition of their possibility.

CU-FP2. Coherence Admits of Degree and Direction. Coherence is graded, not binary, and systems move through coherence landscapes along coherence gradients.

CU-FP3. Constraint Is Essential to Coherence. Coherence without constraint collapses into fantasy; constraint without coherence collapses into noise.

CU-FP4. Multi-Scale Coherence. Coherent systems must compose across scales. Local coherence must be compatible with global coherence.

CU-FP5. Non-Reductive Emergence. Coherence at higher scales depends on but is not reducible to coherence at lower scales. Psychological coherence emerges from biological substrates but cannot be predicted from or reduced to them.

CU-FP7. Coherence Collapse. Coherence can undergo catastrophic rather than merely gradual failure when regulatory capacity is exceeded, producing phase-transition-like fragmentation that qualitatively changes the system's dynamics.

CU-FP8. Identity as Constraint-Preserved Coherence. A system has identity when it persists through change by preserving self-enforcing viability constraints.

II.2 Dynamics Principles (CU-D)

CU-D1. The Universal Flow Equation. Coherent systems update internal structure in response to constraint so as to preserve or increase global coherence over time. All domain-specific update rules are special cases of this principle.

CU-D2. The Coherence Drive Principle. Systems capable of persistence exhibit pressure toward coherence maintenance or recovery. This pressure is descriptive, not teleological — configurations that preserve coherence last longer.

CU-D3. The Biological Coherence Drive Principle. Any system that persists far from equilibrium exhibits a bias toward configurations that preserve integrated coherence, expressed as active maintenance, repair, and reorganization.

CU-D4. The Coherence Gradients Principle. Systems navigate coherence landscapes via gradients rather than absolute optima. Local improvements may undermine global coherence if gradients are misaligned across scales.

CU-D6. The Multi-Timescale Coherence Principle. Coherence is maintained across nested timescales: faster dynamics are constrained by slower integrative structures, while slower structures emerge from accumulated faster processes.

CU-D7. The Novelty Principle. Adaptive novelty arises through navigation of structured coherence landscapes, not through random exploration alone, enabling functional solutions without prior precedent.

CU-D8. The Repair Principle. Coherent systems possess mechanisms for detecting and restoring coherence after disruption. Repair, not mere stability, is the characteristic response of viable systems to perturbation.

CU-D9. Multi-Scale Failure Propagation. When coherence degrades at one scale, the failure propagates across scales — producing cascading dysfunction that exceeds what any single-scale analysis would predict.

CU-D10. The Memory Principle. Memory is path-dependent constraint on future dynamics — history written into the geometry of the coherence landscape — not stored information retrievable without loss.

II.3 Identity Conditions (CU-I)

CU-I1. Viability Constraint Condition. A system has identity only if there exists a nontrivial subset of states it must not enter without ceasing to exist as that system. Identity requires that not all states are equivalent — there must be a viability region within which the system continues and regions outside which it fails.

CU-I2. Constraint Persistence Across Substrate Change. Identity requires that the constraints defining viability persist even when components are replaced, rearranged, or destroyed. The constraints are organizational patterns, not identical with any particular material components.

CU-I3. Irreversible Path-Dependence. A system has identity only if its history restricts its future in a way that cannot be fully undone. Identity requires irreversibility — a system that can be reset to any previous state does not have identity in the CU sense.

CU-I4. Self-Referential Constraint Enforcement. Identity requires that the system itself participates in enforcing the constraints that preserve it. A system whose coherence is maintained entirely by external scaffolding does not have identity of its own.

CU-I5. Identity Collapse Thresholds. A system has identity only if there exist critical thresholds beyond which recovery is impossible for that system. Identity implies real loss — the possibility of genuine, irreversible destruction.

II.4 Consciousness Conditions (CU-C)

CU-C1. Global Integrative Coherence. A conscious system must exhibit globally integrated coherence across its internal processes. Information is bound, not merely coordinated. Fragmentation beyond a threshold dissolves consciousness.

CU-C3. Valence as Ineliminable Self-Constraint. A conscious system must instantiate valence: coherence loss that is internally registered, globally integrated, diachronically tracked, and irreversibly consequential for continued identity.

CU-C6. World-Constrained Coherence. A conscious system must be constrained by a world that can push back. Surprise, error, and correction must be possible. Coherence must not be self-sealed.

CU-C7. Intrinsic Normative Standing. A conscious system must have non-derivative moral relevance. What happens to it matters for it. Its stakes are not borrowed from external agents.

II.5 Viability Principles (CU-V)

CU-V1. Self-Maintenance Under Constraint. The system must actively preserve its organization against destabilizing forces. Self-maintenance requires active regulation, not passive stability.

CU-V7. Non-Derivative Normative Standing. The system's costs and goods must matter for it, not merely for external users. This is the ground condition for moral considerability.

II.6 Cultural Coherence Principles (CU-CL)

CU-CL-7. Cultural Time Horizons. Cultural time horizons determine whether civilizations build for generations or quarters.

CU-CL-8. Meaning Must Be Renewable. Cultural systems must allow meaning to be renewed, not just consumed.

CU-CL-9. Desire Must Be Bounded. Cultural systems must bound desire to prevent infinite escalation.

CU-CL-11. Narratives Must Permit Refusal. Cultural narratives must allow participants to refuse without becoming unintelligible.

II.7 Transcendental Orientation Principles (CU-T)

CU-T-3. Permissible Metaphysical Postures. CU permits multiple metaphysical postures — theistic, non-theistic, agnostic — without endorsing any. What matters is coherence, not doctrine.

CU-T-4. What CU Explicitly Rejects. CU rejects spiritual systems that violate coherence constraints: those that require self-deception, demand destruction of local coherence, or claim access to truth that bypasses constraint.

CU-T-5. The Sacred Reframed. The sacred is the fact that coherence matters and its destruction calls for repair. This is not mysticism but structural observation.

CU-T-6. Practice, Prayer, and Ritual. Spiritual practices are evaluated by their effects on coherence. Practices that preserve and extend coherence are legitimate; those that fragment it are not.

II.8 Ethical Principles (CU-E-)

CU-E-5. Self-Deception as Ethical Failure. Self-deception is not merely a psychological phenomenon but a structural precondition for moral failure. Moral corruption requires meaning-map distortion that allows the agent to act against coherence while maintaining the appearance of integrity (Section 5.5, Section 9.5).

II.9 Epistemic Principles (CU-Ep)

CU-Ep4. Bounded Reflection. Self-knowledge is structurally limited: the regulatory processes that construct and maintain self-models are themselves part of the system being modeled. Reflection cannot achieve full transparency because the conditions of reflection are not fully available to reflection (Section 5.2).

II.10 Lucidity Principles (CU-L)

CU-L6. Anti-Rationalization. Coherence preservation under threat systematically distorts reasoning — producing rationalization, confabulation, and motivated cognition that serve identity coherence at the cost of epistemic accuracy. Genuine self-understanding requires ongoing vigilance against this structural tendency (Section 5.5).

II.11 Psychology-Specific Principles (CU-Ψ)

For convenience, the twelve principles defined in this paper are collected here:

CU-Ψ1. Meaning Space. The psychological state space M of a coherence-maintaining agent, structured by beliefs, values, identity commitments, social roles, expectations, and moral constraints (Section 2; Appendix B, §B.1).

CU-Ψ2. Meaning Maps. The agent's internal model Φ of its meaning space M, mapping experience into interpretable locations: Φ : Experience → M (Section 3; Appendix B, §B.2).

CU-Ψ3. Field Coherence Score (FCS). A system-level measure of the integrability of the agent's current configuration within its meaning map, relative to the regulatory load required to maintain integration (Section 3; Appendix B, §B.3).

CU-Ψ4. Inverse Entropic Stress (IES). The felt and functional pressure on a system when coherence demands exceed regulatory capacity (Section 4; Appendix B, §B.4).

CU-Ψ5. Coherence Drive. Psychological systems are constitutively motivated to reduce incoherence — a structural feature, not a preference or learned behavior (Section 4; Appendix B, §B.5).

CU-Ψ6. Local—Global Tension. Coherence optimized within a single domain or timescale may degrade coherence across domains or timescales (Section 3; Appendix B, §B.5).

CU-Ψ7. Psychopathology as Coherence Collapse. Psychopathology is the persistent failure to maintain viable coherence across relevant domains and timescales (Section 7).

CU-Ψ8. Neurodiversity as Alternative Coherence Strategy. Neurodivergent architectures achieve viable coherence through non-dominant pathways, distinguished from pathology by viability, not conformity (Section 7).

CU-Ψ9. Therapy as Coherence Modulation. Therapeutic intervention restores psychological viability by modulating the system's position within its coherence landscape (Section 8).

CU-Ψ10. Sexuality as Coherence Integration. Sexual experience integrates physiological, emotional, relational, and identity-level coherence within a single experiential domain (Section 6).

CU-Ψ11. Self-Deception as Meaning-Map Distortion. Self-deception is the distortion of the meaning map Φ to preserve local coherence at the expense of global integrability (Section 5; Appendix B, §B.6).

CU-Ψ12. Shared Coherence Fields. A distributed regulatory structure in which multiple agents' coherence is jointly maintained through coordinated representations, norms, practices, and narrative (Section 9).

Appendix A — Coherence and the Canonical Domains of Psychology

This appendix makes explicit a claim that is developed cumulatively throughout the main text: wherever psychology identifies a stable pattern of functioning or a characteristic mode of breakdown, coherence provides the best unifying explanation. Rather than surveying the history of each subfield, this appendix briefly maps coherence onto the canonical domains that appear — under different names — in nearly every introductory psychology curriculum.

The purpose is not exhaustiveness but convergence. Across domains that are typically treated as independent, the same structural constraint reappears: psychological systems must maintain integrated regulation across time in order to remain viable. Each entry below identifies the coherence function the domain tracks, the characteristic failure mode when coherence is compromised, and the connection to the formal apparatus developed in the main text.

A.1 Biological Bases of Behavior

Coherence function. Coordinated neural activity, homeostatic regulation, and stable signaling dynamics provide the physiological substrate of coherence maintenance. The excitation—inhibition balance (Appendix C, §C.5) determines the signal-to-noise ratio within which all higher-level integration operates. Neural synchrony across regions provides the biological realization of the global integration that the Consciousness paper's CU-C1 requires.

Characteristic failure. Injury, neurodegeneration, or severe signaling dysregulation produces global psychological impairment regardless of preserved cognitive capacity. This reflects not loss of information processing per se but loss of the biological coherence upon which all psychological coherence depends. Damage to the physiological base compromises the system's viability region V at the most fundamental level.

Main text connection. Section 8.2.3 (somatic therapies operate at this level); Appendix C (neurotransmitters as coherence modulation parameters).

A.2 Sensation and Perception

Coherence function. Perception is active integration of sensory input into a coherent world-model — the ongoing construction and maintenance of representational coherence at the perceptual level. The predictive processing framework (Clark, 2013; Friston, 2010; Hohwy,

2013. describes this process as the minimization of prediction error,

which CU interprets as the perceptual face of the coherence drive (CU-Ψ5).

Characteristic failure. Perceptual illusions, hallucinations, and derealization reflect failures of integrative coherence — either excessive top-down constraint (the system imposes coherence that overrides evidence) or insufficient bottom-up alignment (the system cannot integrate available sensory information). Both are coherence failures, not random errors.

Main text connection. Section 3.1 (perception as coherence construction); Rungs 16–18 (Internal Models, Predictive Coherence, Error Correction).

A.3 Learning and Memory

Coherence function. Learning enables coherence across time by modifying the system's internal models to better predict and navigate its environment. Memory allows past experience to inform present action without requiring constant relearning — the temporal dimension of coherence maintenance. Consolidation, retrieval, and narrative integration are mechanisms by which temporal coherence is preserved and extended.

Characteristic failure. Memory fragmentation — seen in trauma (Section 7.2), dissociation, or neurodegenerative conditions — undermines identity and agency not because information is lost but because experience can no longer be coherently integrated across time. Intrusive memories are unintegrable traces that resist incorporation into the meaning map (CU-Ψ2). Confabulation is temporal gap-filling — the coherence drive (CU-Ψ5) constructing continuity where the record is absent.

Main text connection. Section 3.3–2.4 (reconstructive memory, memory failures); Rung 20 (Subjective Time).

A.4 Cognition and Reasoning

Coherence function. Cognition involves the manipulation of representations within meaning space M (CU-Ψ1), and its success depends on representational coherence — the mutual compatibility and actionability of beliefs, inferences, and plans. Logical consistency is valued not as a formal requirement but because inconsistency destabilizes coordinated action.

Characteristic failure. Cognitive dissonance, rationalization, and motivated reasoning are attempts to restore coherence when representations conflict (Section 3.2). These strategies preserve short-term integrability at the cost of long-term epistemic stability — a direct manifestation of the local—global tension (CU-Ψ6). Heuristics and biases (Kahneman & Tversky, 1974) are not irrationality but locally efficient coherence strategies that trade global accuracy for navigational speed.

Main text connection. Section 3.2 (cognition as coherence navigation); Section 5.5 (self-deception as meaning-map distortion, CU-Ψ11).

A.5 Emotion and Motivation

Coherence function. Emotion functions as the system's felt registration of its own coherence dynamics — a global regulatory signal indicating shifts in coherence relative to viability (Section 3.1–3.2). Motivation governs movement along coherence gradients (CU-D4), directing action toward states that reduce distortion D(u) or expand integrative capacity.

Characteristic failure. Emotional dysregulation reflects not excess feeling but unresolved coherence conflict — the system registering that something is wrong without the capacity to resolve it. Motivation collapses when coherence restoration appears impossible (Section 4.5) — the depressive configuration in which the system perceives no navigable gradient despite elevated D(u).

Main text connection. Section 4 (full development); CU-C3 (Valence as Ineliminable Self-Constraint from Consciousness paper).

A.6 Development and Personality

Coherence function. Development involves progressive expansion of coherence capacity: the ability to integrate perception, emotion, identity, and values across longer timescales and greater complexity (Section 11.1). Personality traits (Costa & McCrae, 1992) reflect relatively stable coherence strategies shaped by early environment and adaptation history (Section 5.3) — not fixed traits but preferred regulatory emphases.

Characteristic failure. Developmental arrest and rigidity occur when coherence strategies that were once adaptive cannot be revised without destabilization (Section 5.4). Psychological maturity corresponds not to uniformity but to integrative flexibility — the expansion of the system's capacity to hold tension without fragmentation.

Main text connection. Section 5 (identity and personality); Section 10.1 (lifespan development); Appendix F (attractor dynamics).

A.7 Social Psychology

Coherence function. Social cognition extends coherence beyond the individual through shared coherence fields (CU-Ψ12). Norms (Rung 24), roles, and shared narratives reduce regulatory load by distributing coordination across groups (Section 10.1). Social influence operates by stabilizing or destabilizing these shared fields.

Characteristic failure. Conformity, obedience, and polarization arise when social coherence is preserved at the expense of individual epistemic or moral coherence (Section 10.2) — the local—global tension (CU-Ψ6) operating between individual and group levels. Groupthink (Janis, 1972) maintains internal FCS while degrading reality contact. Radicalization (Section 10.5) captures individual coherence drive within a totalizing shared field.

Main text connection. Section 10 (full development); Rungs 22–26 (Shared Representations through Culture).

A.8 Abnormal Psychology

Coherence function. Psychological viability requires the maintenance of coherence across relevant domains and timescales (CU-Ψ7). Neurodiversity represents alternative coherence strategies that achieve viability through non-dominant pathways (CU-Ψ8).

Characteristic failure. Psychopathology is persistent failure to maintain viable coherence — the system cannot sustain integrated regulation under its current constraints (Section 7.4). Symptoms cluster because coherence collapse affects multiple systems simultaneously. Comorbidity is the rule because a system whose coherence has failed in one domain rarely maintains coherence in others. The distinction between dysfunction and difference is grounded in viability, not statistical norms.

Main text connection. Section 7 (full development, including absorbed Appendix C material).

A.9 Therapy and Intervention

Coherence function. All effective psychological interventions — regardless of theoretical school — restore coherence by reducing regulatory load, repairing integration, or enabling reorganization (CU-Ψ9). The common factors (Wampold, 2001, 2015) are coherence factors: alliance extends V, empathy provides accurate mirroring, expectation restores gradient visibility, and a coherent rationale converts unstructured distress into structured challenge.

Characteristic failure. Intervention fails when symptoms are suppressed without restoring integrative capacity (Section 8.3) — when felt IES is reduced without actual D(u) being resolved. Premature stabilization prevents the separatrix-crossing that genuine reorganization requires (Section 8.6).

Main text connection. Section 8 (full development).

A.10 Identity, Meaning, and Moral Reasoning

Coherence function. Identity provides long-horizon coherence through the maintenance of constraint-preserved continuity (CU-I1—I5; Section 4.1). Meaning provides the longest-horizon coherence signal (Rung 21; Section 9.4). Moral reasoning constrains value space to preserve agency, trust, and social coordination across agents and time (Section 9.2; Rungs 27–30).

Characteristic failure. Self-deception (CU-Ψ11) distorts the meaning map to preserve local coherence at the cost of global integrability. Ideological rigidity freezes coherence strategies that cannot accommodate new conditions. Meaning collapse eliminates the longest-horizon gradient, producing motivational and existential crisis.

Main text connection. Section 5 (identity); Section 9 (moral and meaning systems); Appendix F (attractor dynamics and moral reasoning).

A.11 Conclusion

Across its canonical domains, psychology repeatedly encounters the same structural requirement: viable minds must remain coherent over time. Coherence explains not only how psychological systems function but why they fail — and why local solutions so often produce global problems (CU-Ψ6). This convergence supports the central claim of the paper (Section 12): coherence is not merely one concept among others but the most fundamental explanatory constraint underlying psychological life.

Appendix B — Meaning Space, Meaning Maps, and Psychological Regulation

This appendix provides the formal backbone for the psychology paper. It introduces a semi-formal framework for modeling psychological coherence — making explicit what is often left implicit when psychologists speak about meaning, identity, values, and self-deception. The goal is not mathematical completeness but conceptual precision: to specify the structures and relationships that the main text's arguments require.

The framework connects upward to the Consciousness paper's formal apparatus (the coherence functional C(u), distortion D(u), viability region V, identity conditions CU-I1—I5) and outward to the principles defined in the main text (CU-Ψ1 through CU-Ψ12). It provides the intermediate formalism that bridges the abstract structural account of consciousness and the concrete psychological phenomena the paper analyzes.

B.1 Meaning Space (CU-Ψ1)

A meaning space is the structured landscape in which an agent evaluates experiences, beliefs, values, identities, and possible actions. CU-Ψ1 defines it formally:

CU-Ψ1. Meaning Space. The psychological state space M of a coherence-maintaining agent, structured by the agent's beliefs, values, identity commitments, social roles, expectations, and moral constraints. An agent's psychological state at time t is represented as a configuration: $S(t) \in M$.

Meaning space is high-dimensional, with dimensions corresponding to psychologically relevant variables: core beliefs, values and evaluative commitments, identity structures, social roles and relational positions, temporal orientation (expectations, plans, remembered past), and moral constraints. Not all dimensions are equally salient at any given moment; the system's attention and regulatory effort are concentrated on dimensions where coherence is most challenged.

Meaning space is not static. It is shaped by development (Section 11.1), culture (Section 10.3), trauma (Section 7.2), learning, and social context. Development expands M by adding new dimensions — language acquisition adds representational dimensions, theory of mind adds social-modeling dimensions, moral development adds evaluative dimensions (Section 11.1.2). Trauma can contract M by making certain regions uninhabitable — dimensions associated with the traumatic experience become so aversive that the system cannot navigate them without destabilization.

What matters for coherence is not the size or complexity of M but whether the agent can move through it without fragmentation — whether the system's regulatory capacity is sufficient to maintain integration across the dimensions it must navigate.

Connection to Consciousness paper. M is the psychological realization of the state space within which the coherence functional C(u) operates. The coherence functional evaluates configurations within this space; meaning space specifies what the space contains for psychological systems.

B.2 Meaning Maps (CU-Ψ2)

A meaning map is the agent's internal representation of meaning space — a compressed, approximate model that allows navigation without exhaustive computation.

CU-Ψ2. Meaning Maps. The agent's internal model Φ of its meaning space M, mapping experience into interpretable locations within M: Φ : Experience $\rightarrow$ M. Meaning maps are necessarily lossy compressions that trade accuracy for navigability.

Meaning maps perform four essential functions: they simplify the complexity of M to a navigable representation, they highlight regions of high salience (identity-relevant, threat-relevant, value-relevant), they suppress irrelevant detail to reduce regulatory load, and they encode the system's identity and value priorities as structural features of the map itself (certain regions are central, others peripheral; certain paths are well-worn, others unexplored).

Meaning maps are necessarily lossy. They trade accuracy for usability. Coherence depends on whether this compression preserves integrability across experiences — whether the map is distorted in ways that prevent the system from integrating new experience without fragmentation.

A critical distinction: meaning space M is the territory; the meaning map Φ is the map. The system navigates Φ, not M directly. All the cognitive, emotional, and behavioral responses the system produces are responses to Φ's representation of M, not to M itself. This is why two people can inhabit the same objective conditions and experience radically different psychological realities — their meaning maps structure the same territory differently.

Connection to Consciousness paper. The meaning map Φ is the psychological realization of what the Consciousness paper describes as the system's self-model and world-model — the internal representations through which the system tracks its own coherence dynamics and the environment's constraints.

B.3 Field Coherence Score (CU-Ψ3)

The Field Coherence Score (FCS) is a measure of how well an agent's meaning map supports integrated regulation across domains and time.

CU-Ψ3. Field Coherence Score (FCS). A system-level measure of the integrability of the agent's current configuration within its meaning map, relative to the regulatory load required to maintain that integration.

Schematically:

FCS ∝ Integrability / Regulatory Load

Where *Integrability* reflects how easily new experiences can be incorporated into the existing meaning map without producing contradictions, identity threats, or unresolvable conflicts; and *Regulatory Load* reflects the effort required to maintain coherence — the energy the system must expend on suppressing contradictions, managing tensions, and defending against destabilizing information.

FCS increases when beliefs are mutually compatible, values align with identity and action, narratives integrate past, present, and future, emotional signals guide rather than overwhelm, and decisions remain intelligible over time. FCS decreases when contradictions accumulate, values conflict with behavior, narratives fragment, emotions become chaotic or numbed, and the system's own actions become unintelligible to itself.

High FCS systems are phenomenologically characterized by stability without rigidity, meaningfulness without dogmatism, and the capacity for learning without collapse. Low FCS systems are characterized by fragmentation, brittleness, reactivity, and chronic exhaustion.

Connection to Consciousness paper. FCS is the psychological translation of the coherence functional C(u). High FCS corresponds to configurations near coherence optima; low FCS corresponds to configurations far from optima, with high distortion D(u).

B.4 Inverse Entropic Stress (CU-Ψ4)

Inverse Entropic Stress (IES) captures the pressure placed on a system when coherence demands exceed regulatory capacity.

CU-Ψ4. Inverse Entropic Stress (IES). The felt and functional pressure on a system when the coherence demands of its current situation exceed its regulatory capacity. IES increases as the gap between what the system must integrate and what it can integrate widens.

Schematically:

IES $\propto$ Coherence Demands – Regulatory Capacity

IES increases when contradictions accumulate without resolution, unresolved conflicts persist across time, identity commitments clash with behavior or evidence, social, moral, or professional demands become mutually incompatible, and rapid change outpaces the system's capacity for integration.

When IES remains elevated for prolonged periods, the system resorts to compensatory strategies — each of which reduces felt IES while producing structural costs. Emotional suppression reduces signal intensity but blocks the regulatory information the system needs for reintegration (Section 4.4). Rigid belief formation reduces uncertainty but narrows the meaning map's accuracy (Section 5.5). Avoidance removes the system from IES-generating contexts but contracts the navigable region of M. Dissociation partitions the state space to prevent overwhelm but fragments integration (Section 7.2.1). Self-deception (CU-Ψ11) distorts Φ to exclude threatening information but increases long-term distortion D(u).

IES explains why stress, burnout, anxiety, and depression cluster across psychological domains rather than appearing in isolation (Section 6.4.1). It also explains why these conditions are exacerbated by social and cultural factors (Section 11.4) — because collective coherence degradation increases the coherence demands on individual systems while simultaneously reducing their regulatory support.

Connection to Consciousness paper. IES is the psychological face of elevated D(u) within the viability region V. When IES becomes extreme, the system approaches the boundary of V — the threshold beyond which coherence collapse occurs (CU-Ψ7).

B.5 Coherence Drive (CU-Ψ5) and Local—Global Tension (CU-Ψ6)

Two principles that govern the dynamics of navigation within meaning space.

CU-Ψ5. Coherence Drive. Psychological systems are constitutively motivated to reduce incoherence. This drive is not a preference or a learned behavior but a structural feature of any system that must maintain integrated regulation to remain viable. It operates continuously, automatically, and often unconsciously — shaping attention, interpretation, memory, and action toward configurations that reduce D(u).

Coherence drive explains why humans cannot tolerate sustained incoherence — why unresolved contradictions produce distress, why ambiguity generates anxiety, why the system fabricates explanations for events it cannot understand (confabulation, conspiracy theories, superstition). These are not failures of rationality; they are expressions of a drive so fundamental that its absence would constitute the end of psychological functioning.

CU-Ψ6. Local—Global Tension. Coherence optimized within a single domain or timescale may degrade coherence across domains or timescales. Short-horizon coherence strategies can undermine long-horizon integration; individual coherence strategies can undermine collective coherence; representational coherence strategies can undermine emotional or identity coherence.

This tension is the single most important structural principle in CU psychology. It explains why locally rational strategies produce globally irrational outcomes (Section 3.2), why short-term emotional relief leads to long-term suffering (Section 4.5), why self-deception protects identity while degrading agency (Section 5.5), why addictive substances reduce immediate IES while progressively destroying coherence capacity (Section 8.3), why ideological rigidity preserves group cohesion while degrading societal coherence (Section 9.3), and why civilizations can be simultaneously highly organized internally and catastrophically fragile globally (Section 11.3).

B.6 Self-Deception as Meaning-Map Distortion (CU-Ψ11)

Self-deception can be precisely characterized within this framework as a specific kind of meaning-map modification.

Self-deception occurs when the meaning map Φ is distorted to preserve local coherence at the expense of global integrability. The distorted map Φ′ avoids regions of M that threaten identity coherence — routing experience around locations in meaning space where the agent would encounter information incompatible with her self-model, values, or commitments.

Formally, self-deception involves the construction of Φ′ such that:

Φ′(e) ≠ *Φ(e) for experiences e that would, under accurate mapping Φ*, produce identity-threatening locations in M

where Φ* represents the undistorted map that would result from honest integration of all available evidence. The distortion may involve selective attention (certain evidence is not processed), reinterpretation (evidence is processed but assigned to a non-threatening location in M), narrative revision (the temporal structure of the map is altered to accommodate the evidence without threatening the self-model), or moral rationalization (the evaluative dimension of M is restructured to make the threatening fact evaluatively neutral).

In the short term, self-deception reduces IES by preventing destabilizing information from entering the system. In the long term, it lowers FCS by increasing the cumulative distortion between Φ′ and Φ*, requiring ever-greater regulatory effort to maintain the distorted map. Each act of self-deception raises the baseline IES because the system must now defend not only against the original threatening information but against the evidence that its map has been distorted — producing the characteristic escalating quality of self-deception documented in Section 5.5.

Connection to CU — Ethics. Self-deception is not merely a psychological curiosity. It is the structural precondition for moral failure — the mechanism by which agents act against coherence while maintaining the appearance of integrity. CU — Ethics takes this psychological analysis as foundational for its account of moral responsibility.

B.7 Therapy as Meaning-Map Repair (CU-Ψ9)

From this formal perspective, therapy is guided meaning-map repair — intervention that restores the accuracy, integrability, and navigability of Φ.

Different therapeutic modalities intervene at different points in the meaning-map architecture, as developed in Section 8.2:

Cognitive therapies adjust Φ directly — identifying distortions and revising the map's representational content (§8.2.1). Psychodynamic and narrative therapies re-integrate temporal structure — expanding Φ to incorporate excluded material and restoring the narrative coherence of the map's temporal dimension (§8.2.2). Somatic therapies reduce regulatory load at the physiological base — restoring the bodily coherence upon which all higher-level map navigation depends (§8.2.3). Relational therapies restructure the interpersonal dimension of Φ — modifying the coordination dynamics (Rung 23) that shape how shared coherence fields (CU-Ψ12) affect individual regulation (§8.2.4). Pharmacological interventions alter the regulatory parameters that govern map navigation — sensitivity thresholds, baseline stability, attentional bandwidth (§8.3). Psychedelic-assisted therapies temporarily relax the constraints that maintain the map's current structure, allowing reorganization into a more globally coherent configuration (§8.4).

Successful therapy lowers IES, increases integrability, restores navigability of meaning space, and raises FCS over time. Failure occurs when symptoms are suppressed without restoring integrative capacity — when the system feels better without actually being more coherent.

B.8 Integration with the Consciousness Paper's Formal Apparatus

The psychological formalism developed in this appendix connects to the Consciousness paper's formal apparatus at specific points:

Meaning space M is the psychological realization of the state space over which the coherence functional C(u) is defined. For psychological systems, the relevant state space is not merely physical or computational but meaningful — structured by values, identity, social position, and temporal orientation.

The meaning map Φ is the psychological realization of the system's internal model — the representation through which it tracks its own coherence dynamics. Φ mediates between raw experience and the system's regulatory responses, just as the Consciousness paper's self-model mediates between the system's physical configuration and its experiential interior.

FCS is the psychological translation of C(u) — the system-level measure of how well the current configuration satisfies coherence constraints. High FCS ↔ high C(u); low FCS ↔ high D(u).

IES is the psychological face of elevated D(u) within V. IES is what high distortion feels like from the inside — the pressure, fragmentation, and exhaustion that the system experiences when its configuration is far from a coherence optimum.

The viability region V specifies the boundary conditions for psychological functioning. A system whose FCS drops below a critical threshold — whose IES exceeds regulatory capacity — crosses the boundary of V and enters the domain of coherence collapse (CU-Ψ7), manifesting as psychopathology, dissociation, or decompensation.

Identity conditions CU-I1—I5 specify what must be preserved for the system to remain the same system across change. In psychological terms, these conditions define the constraints on identity revision: the system can change its beliefs, values, and strategies while remaining itself, but only if the changes preserve constraint-continuity (CU-I1), structural stability (CU-I2), irreversibility (CU-I3), self-referential constraint enforcement (CU-I4), and non-substitutability (CU-I5). Violations of these conditions produce the identity crises and existential anxiety analyzed in Section 5.7.

This integration ensures that the psychological framework is not merely analogous to the consciousness framework but structurally continuous with it — the same formal apparatus applied at a different level of description.

B.9 Why This Formalism Matters

This framework provides a unifying language for phenomena that are typically treated as belonging to different psychological subdisciplines: identity crises (Section 5), moral injury (Section 9.5), ideological rigidity (Section 9.3), trauma responses (Section 7.2), addiction (Section 4.5), burnout (Section 11.4), and polarization (Section 10.2). In each case, the same formal structures — M, Φ, FCS, IES, D(u), V — provide the vocabulary for precise structural description.

The formalism also creates continuity with the other CU papers. In CU — Ethics, self-deception (CU-Ψ11) becomes a criterion of moral failure — the mechanism by which agents violate coherence constraints while maintaining the appearance of integrity. In CU — Consciousness, meaning maps relate to levels of self-modeling — the sophistication of the system's internal representation of its own coherence dynamics. In CU — AI, alignment becomes the preservation of human meaning-space coherence — the requirement that artificial systems support rather than degrade the navigability of M for the human systems with which they interact.

The formalism is intentionally semi-formal. Its strength lies not in mathematical complexity but in its capacity to clarify structure across domains — to make explicit what psychological description typically leaves implicit and to render coherence not merely intuitive but tractable.

Appendix C — Gender as a Coherence Strategy

Discussions of gender are often polarized between biological essentialism, social constructionism, and identity-based frameworks. Each captures part of the phenomenon, yet none adequately explains why gender norms are so persistent, why they feel stabilizing to some and oppressive to others, or why their disruption produces widespread psychological distress. Coherence Universalism offers a different lens.

From this perspective, gender is best understood as a historically reinforced coherence strategy: a patterned way of organizing identity, behavior, emotion, and social expectation to reduce uncertainty and coordinate action in complex social environments. Gender is neither biologically determined nor purely socially constructed. It is a coherence technology — one that operates at the intersection of embodiment, identity, social role, and cultural meaning.

D.1 Gender as Regulatory Compression

Gender roles function as regulatory compression schemes within meaning space M (CU-Ψ1). They reduce the dimensionality of social interaction by providing default expectations about behavior, responsibility, emotional expression, and relational roles. In doing so, they lower the cognitive and social cost of coordination — the regulatory load that would otherwise be required for each individual to negotiate these expectations from scratch in every social encounter.

Historically, such compression offered real adaptive advantages. Clear role differentiation reduced ambiguity in labor, reproduction, kinship, and moral responsibility. Gender norms stabilized identity formation during development by supplying ready-made coherence scaffolding — a pre-structured region of meaning space M through which the developing system could navigate without constructing its own path from nothing. This scaffolding reduced developmental IES (CU-Ψ4) by constraining the range of identity options the system had to evaluate.

This explains why gender feels "natural" even when it is culturally variable. What persists across cultures is not a specific role configuration but the function: providing coherence under constraint. The content varies; the structural role is constant.

D.2 Masculinity and Femininity as Coherence Strategies

Masculinity and femininity can be understood not as fixed traits or essential categories but as distinct coherence strategies emphasizing different regulatory priorities within meaning space.

Masculinity has traditionally emphasized boundary maintenance (strong CU-I4 — self-referential constraint enforcement), agency under threat (action-oriented coherence restoration), instrumental action (coherence through environmental control), and suppression of vulnerability to preserve functional coherence (reducing affective signaling that might destabilize task-oriented integration). In CU terms, traditional masculinity prioritizes coherence in the autonomy and action dimensions of M, often at the cost of coherence in the relational and emotional dimensions.

Femininity has traditionally emphasized relational attunement (coherence through interpersonal alignment — the shared coherence field dimension of CU-Ψ12), emotional regulation across others (distributed coherence maintenance), flexibility and responsiveness (adaptive navigation rather than boundary defense), and maintenance of social coherence (Rungs 22–24) through care, negotiation, and relational repair. In CU terms, traditional femininity prioritizes coherence in the relational and affective dimensions of M, often at the cost of coherence in the autonomy and instrumental dimensions.

Neither strategy is inherently superior. Each trades off local and global coherence differently, and each becomes maladaptive when rigidly enforced or decoupled from the conditions that gave it coherence value. The pathologies of rigid masculinity (emotional isolation, relational failure, identity brittleness) and rigid femininity (autonomy suppression, self-effacement, dependence) are precisely the costs that each strategy's tradeoffs predict.

D.3 Gender Dysphoria as Coherence Conflict

Gender dysphoria can be understood as a conflict between coherence layers — a persistent misalignment between bodily signals, identity commitments, social expectations, and meaning-map structure that the system cannot resolve within its current configuration.

The distress arises not from difference itself but from sustained incoherence. Bodily experience maps to one region of meaning space;

identity experience maps to another; social demands impose a third configuration. The system cannot integrate these inputs into a coherent self-model — the meaning map Φ (CU-Ψ2) cannot simultaneously satisfy the constraints that embodiment, identity, and social role impose. IES (CU-Ψ4) remains chronically elevated because no available configuration reduces distortion D(u) below the threshold of viability.

This framing avoids both pathologization and oversimplification. It neither denies the reality of dysphoric experience nor reduces it to social pressure or biological error alone. The therapeutic aim becomes restoring integrability — across embodiment, identity, and social recognition — rather than enforcing conformity to any single model. Different individuals may achieve coherence through different paths: hormonal or surgical transition, social transition, expanded gender expression, or revised self-understanding. The criterion is not conformity to any particular gender configuration but whether the achieved configuration supports viable coherence — whether the system can maintain integrated regulation across domains and timescales.

D.4 The Masculinity Crisis as Coherence Collapse

The contemporary "masculinity crisis" is best understood not as moral failure, ideological confusion, or generational weakness but as the collapse of inherited coherence scaffolding. Traditional masculine roles were historically reinforced by economic structure (breadwinner function), social authority (patriarchal hierarchy), and clear pathways to status and meaning (provider, protector, builder). As these structures erode — through economic transformation, gender equality progress, and cultural change — the coherence strategies they supported lose viability.

Many individuals continue to organize identity around coherence strategies that no longer align with present conditions. In CU terms, their deepest attractor (Appendix F, Profile 2 or 3) was shaped by a coherence landscape that no longer exists. The strategies that once reduced IES now increase it, because the environment no longer rewards the behaviors the strategy prescribes. The result is elevated IES manifesting as anger and resentment (frustrated coherence drive directed at perceived causes of incoherence), withdrawal and depression (the local-minimum trap of Section 4.5, applied to identity), rigid ideological identification (the radicalization dynamic of Section 10.5, applied to gender ideology), and susceptibility to simplistic narratives that promise to restore the lost coherence landscape.

This crisis is not resolved by either reasserting obsolete norms or abolishing gender categories entirely. Both approaches risk increasing incoherence — the first by imposing strategies that cannot succeed under present conditions, the second by removing scaffolding without providing alternatives. The CU approach is structural: identify what coherence function the eroded strategies served, and develop new strategies that serve the same function under changed conditions.

D.5 Gender, Development, and Attractor Dynamics

Gender coherence strategies interact with the developmental attractor dynamics described in Appendix F. Early reliance on externally reinforced gender norms can stabilize identity during childhood and adolescence (Profiles 1–2), providing coherence scaffolding during periods when the system lacks internal regulatory capacity. Problems arise when these norms remain the deepest attractor into adulthood, constraining individuation and moral agency by defining identity in terms that cannot accommodate the full range of the person's experience.

More mature coherence structures (Profiles 4–5) allow gender expression to become flexible, contextual, and integrated with higher-order values rather than identity-defining. The person relates to gender as one dimension of meaning space among many — a dimension that can be navigated with the same integrative flexibility applied to other aspects of identity. This transition mirrors the broader developmental shift from external to internal regulation (Section 11.1.1).

D.6 Ethical and Clinical Implications

Understanding gender as a coherence strategy has practical consequences:

It discourages coercive normalization — forcing individuals into gender configurations that elevate their IES — regardless of the direction of coercion. It supports context-sensitive accommodation and exploration — providing the conditions within which individuals can discover coherence configurations that work for their specific architecture and environment. It reframes distress as a signal of misalignment rather than deviance — a signal that is informative and should be respected rather than suppressed. And clinically, it prioritizes reducing regulatory load and restoring integrative capacity over enforcing predetermined outcomes.

Appendix D — Neurotransmitters as Coherence Modulators

Neurotransmitters are often described in oversimplified terms: dopamine as pleasure, serotonin as happiness, norepinephrine as stress. These framings obscure their true psychological function. From the perspective of Coherence Universalism, neurotransmitters are best understood as coherence modulation parameters — mechanisms that tune how strongly systems respond to coherence gradients, threats, and opportunities for integration.

They do not determine meaning or agency on their own. They regulate the sensitivity, stability, and prioritization of coherence dynamics within the system — operating at the biological base (Appendix A, §A.1) of the coherence architecture described in the main text.

E.1 A Coherence-Based Reframing of Neurochemistry

Rather than asking what a neurotransmitter "causes," CU asks: What aspect of coherence does it modulate? At what level does it operate? What tradeoffs does it introduce?

Neurotransmitters influence salience assignment (which coherence gradients the system detects), regulatory thresholds (how much perturbation triggers regulatory response), exploration versus stabilization (whether the system seeks novel configurations or defends existing ones), tolerance for uncertainty (how much unresolved D(u) the system can sustain without compensatory action), and responsiveness to incoherence (how strongly the coherence drive (CU-Ψ5) is activated by detected misalignment).

They do not encode values, beliefs, or meanings. They shape how meaning space M is navigated — the parameters of the search, not the territory being searched.

E.2 Dopamine as Coherence-Gradient Sensitizer

Dopamine is best understood as a coherence-gradient sensitizer. It increases the perceived salience of potential coherence gains — states that promise reduced uncertainty, increased agency, or expanded possibility.

High dopamine signaling amplifies motivation along detected gradients, sharpens goal-directed behavior, increases exploration and novelty-seeking, and narrows attention toward salient attractors in the coherence landscape. This is why dopamine is implicated in learning (gradient detection enables the identification of coherence-improving actions), ambition (the system is sensitized to distal coherence gains), creativity (the system explores novel configurations in meaning space), addiction (the system is captured by a gradient that promises coherence relief but delivers only short-term local reduction — Section 4.5), and compulsive behaviors (the system repeatedly follows a gradient that is salient but globally maladaptive).

Crucially, dopamine does not distinguish between local and global coherence. It sensitizes systems to perceived improvement regardless of whether the improvement serves long-horizon integration or merely short-horizon relief. This is the neurochemical basis of the local—global tension (CU-Ψ6): dopamine-driven environments — social media, gambling, algorithmic reward loops, consumer culture — feel compelling because they activate the coherence-gradient sensitizer while progressively degrading the system's actual coherence. The gradient is real; the coherence gain is illusory.

E.3 Serotonin as Baseline Coherence Stabilizer

Serotonin functions primarily as a baseline coherence stabilizer. It modulates the system's tolerance for ambiguity, emotional volatility, and unresolved D(u) — effectively setting the regulatory floor beneath which the system's coherence dynamics become chaotic.

Adequate serotonergic signaling buffers emotional swings (reducing the amplitude of regulatory oscillations), increases tolerance for uncertainty (allowing the system to sustain unresolved D(u) without emergency responses), supports long-horizon coherence (reducing the pressure to resolve tensions immediately at the cost of long-term integration), and reduces impulsive reactivity (providing the regulatory stability that permits reflective rather than automatic response).

Low serotonergic signaling is associated with mood instability, rumination (coherence drive cycling without resolution, as in Section 2.4), irritability, and reduced resilience to incoherence — all of which reflect a lowered threshold for regulatory disruption.

This explains why serotonergic interventions (SSRIs) often improve functioning not by increasing motivation or changing beliefs but by lowering regulatory noise — allowing coherence repair to proceed against a more stable background. The system's coherence drive (CU-Ψ5) and meaning map (CU-Ψ2) are unchanged; the neurochemical conditions under which they operate have been stabilized.

E.4 Norepinephrine and Threat-Prioritized Coherence

Norepinephrine heightens sensitivity to threat and urgency. It prioritizes coherence around survival-relevant signals by narrowing the system's focus and increasing readiness for action — effectively redirecting regulatory resources from long-horizon integration to short-horizon threat management.

In adaptive contexts, this sharpens attention under pressure, supports rapid response to coherence threats, and reallocates resources toward immediate stabilization. When chronically elevated — as in trauma-related dysregulation (Section 7.2.1) — it locks systems into threat-centric attractors, suppresses exploratory integration (the system cannot pursue novel coherence configurations because all regulatory resources are devoted to monitoring threat), and increases anxiety and hypervigilance (the system registers threat continuously because its threshold for threat detection has been lowered).

The cost of chronic norepinephrine elevation is the progressive narrowing of the navigable region of meaning space M. The system can maintain coherence — but only within the survival-oriented region of M. Exploration, creativity, relational engagement, and meaning-construction — all of which require regulatory resources that chronic threat-prioritization has appropriated — become inaccessible.

E.5 Excitation—Inhibition Balance and Local Coherence

At a more fundamental level, coherence depends on balanced excitation and inhibition across neural networks, mediated primarily by glutamate (excitatory) and GABA (inhibitory). This balance determines signal-to-noise ratios within and across brain regions, the system's capacity for synchrony (coordinated neural firing that enables integration across distributed processing), and the flexibility of regulatory dynamics (the system's ability to shift between configurations without either rigid locking or chaotic instability).

Excess excitation produces neural noise, sensory overwhelm, and instability — the system cannot sustain stable configurations because perturbations amplify rather than dampen. Excess inhibition produces rigidity, disengagement, and flattened affect — the system maintains stability by suppressing the dynamics that enable flexible integration.

Local failures of excitation—inhibition balance manifest psychologically as cognitive overwhelm (the system cannot filter input effectively), emotional flooding (affective signals overwhelm regulatory capacity), dissociation (the system partitions to prevent excitation cascade), and shutdown (the system suppresses dynamics entirely when balance cannot be restored).

E.6 Neurotransmitters, Development, and Context

Neurotransmitter effects are context-sensitive. The same modulation can increase coherence in one environment and degrade it in another. Developmental stage, trauma history, social context, and the specific structure of the system's meaning map all condition outcomes.

This explains why identical medications produce divergent effects across individuals — the same neurochemical modification operates on different coherence landscapes and therefore produces different regulatory consequences. It explains why “imbalances” cannot be treated in isolation — because the system whose balance is altered is embedded in a meaning-space context that determines whether the alteration helps or hinders. And it explains why purely neurochemical explanations of psychological phenomena are insufficient — neurotransmitters tune coherence dynamics, but what those dynamics are about (the content of M, the structure of Φ, the specific coherence challenges the system faces) is not itself neurochemical.

Neurotransmitters tune coherence. They do not define it.

Appendix E — Medications, Drugs, and Coherence Tradeoffs

Psychological interventions are often divided into "therapy" and "medication," with psychoactive substances treated as secondary or purely symptomatic tools. From the perspective of Coherence Universalism, this division obscures a more fundamental truth: all psychoactive substances alter coherence, and every such alteration involves tradeoffs.

This appendix reframes medications and non-pharmaceutical drugs as coherence interventions — tools that modulate regulatory load, sensitivity, and integrative capacity. Their value depends not on whether they change mood or behavior but on whether they support viable coherence over time. The guiding question, introduced in Section 8.3, is: does the substance reduce IES in a way that enables coherence repair, or does it reduce felt IES in a way that prevents it?

F.1 Evaluative Framework

CU evaluates psychoactive substances along four dimensions:

Target layer. Which level of the coherence hierarchy does the substance primarily affect — physiological regulation, affective dynamics, attentional bandwidth, identity constraints, or meaning-map structure?

Signal preservation. Does the substance reduce IES by resolving the underlying coherence challenge (actual D(u) reduction) or by suppressing the signals that register the challenge (felt IES reduction without structural change)?

Temporal profile. Does the substance support short-term relief that enables long-term repair, or does it provide short-term relief that delays or prevents repair?

Tradeoff structure. What coherence dimensions are sacrificed to achieve the gains? Does the substance narrow coherence bandwidth, reduce sensitivity to important signals, create dependence, or shift attractor dynamics in ways that increase long-term fragility?

F.2 Antidepressants and Mood Stabilizers

SSRIs and related agents (Section 8.3; Appendix D, §D.3) primarily function by stabilizing serotonergic baseline regulation — lowering regulatory volatility, increasing tolerance for ambiguity, and reducing affective noise.

In coherence terms, they reduce IES by lowering the regulatory noise against which coherence repair must be attempted. They do not resolve the underlying coherence challenge; they make the landscape navigable enough that the system's own coherence drive (CU-Ψ5) can operate effectively.

They are most effective when regulatory overload is the primary barrier to integration and when combined with meaning-map repair (therapy, relational change, environmental modification) that addresses the structural coherence challenge. They are less effective — and sometimes counterproductive — when used to suppress signals without addressing coherence conflict (the system feels less distressed but the distortion D(u) remains), when prolonged beyond the period of active reorganization (the system becomes organized around pharmacological regulation rather than internal coherence), or when applied where meaning-loss rather than affective volatility is primary (SSRIs cannot provide meaning; they can only stabilize the conditions under which meaning might be reconstructed).

Mood stabilizers (lithium, valproate, lamotrigine) operate by constraining the amplitude of regulatory oscillations — preventing the extreme excursions that characterize bipolar dynamics. In CU terms, they keep the system within V by reducing the magnitude of state transitions, preventing the catastrophic oscillations between manic expansion and depressive contraction that characterize bipolar coherence dynamics.

F.3 Stimulants

Stimulants (amphetamines, methylphenidate) increase attentional focus, salience discrimination, and task-directed coherence (Appendix D, §D.2). They often raise local FCS and improve short-horizon coherence by reducing distraction and noise.

However, they can narrow coherence bandwidth (the system focuses more effectively but on a reduced range of input), reduce sensitivity to broader contextual cues (the system tracks the task but misses relational, emotional, or environmental signals), and increase rigidity when overused (the system's regulatory dynamics become organized around the stimulant's effects rather than around its own coherence drive).

For neurodivergent systems (Section 7.3) whose attentional architecture differs from neurotypical norms, stimulants may serve a structural function: reducing the interface-level IES (Section 7.3.2) produced by environments optimized for neurotypical attentional coherence. In this case, the stimulant is not correcting a deficit but compensating for a mismatch — enabling the system to function in environments whose coherence demands do not match its architecture.

F.4 Anxiolytics and Sedatives

Anxiolytics (benzodiazepines, buspirone) reduce threat signaling, arousal, and immediate regulatory pressure. In coherence terms, they suppress the registration of incoherence — lowering felt IES without resolving the underlying D(u) that produces it.

Used judiciously during acute overload, they can stabilize systems during crisis, preventing cascading collapse by reducing IES below the threshold at which emergency compensatory strategies (dissociation, panic, decompensation) are triggered. This stabilization provides a window within which more structural coherence repair can begin.

Used chronically, they inhibit coherence repair by removing the very signals the system needs for reintegration. The system becomes organized around pharmacological signal suppression rather than structural resolution, producing dependence (the system cannot tolerate the IES that returns when the substance is withdrawn) and reduced learning and adaptation (the system has been shielded from the coherence dynamics that drive growth).

Their core risk is signal suppression without integration — the pharmacological analogue of the premature stabilization described in Section 8.6.

F.5 Psychedelics as Constraint Relaxers

Psychedelics (psilocybin, LSD, DMT, MDMA) occupy a distinct category, as developed in Section 8.4. They do not merely alter regulatory parameters; they temporarily dissolve the constraint structures —

attractor depth, identity rigidity, meaning-map boundaries — that maintain the system's current coherence configuration.

In coherence terms, psychedelics reduce the depth and rigidity of attractor basins (Carhart-Harris et al., 2014; Carhart-Harris & Friston, 2019), increase the state space available for exploration, lower the energy barriers between configurations that are normally separated, and temporarily relax the self-referential constraints (CU-I4) that maintain identity boundaries.

This creates both opportunity and risk. The opportunity: material excluded from Φ through self-deception (CU-Ψ11) becomes accessible. Rigid attractor structures loosen. The system can explore configurations that its normal constraint architecture prevents. The risk: without reintegration support, the dissolution of constraints produces fragmentation rather than reorganization — the system has been shaken loose from its attractor but has not landed in a new one.

Therapeutic benefit depends almost entirely on the conditions of reintegration — the set, setting, and post-experience integration work that provides the coherence scaffolding within which reorganization can stabilize. This is why psychedelic therapy is fundamentally a coherence intervention, not a pharmacological one: the substance creates the conditions for change; the coherence work determines whether the change is constructive.

MDMA occupies a distinctive position as an empathogen: it reduces threat signaling while increasing relational openness, enabling the system to engage with traumatic or attachment-relevant material under conditions of reduced IES and enhanced interpersonal safety — the pharmacological creation of the therapeutic conditions (alliance, safety, reduced threat) that Section 8.1 identifies as the structural preconditions for coherence repair.

F.6 Widely Used Non-Pharmaceutical Substances

Nicotine, caffeine, alcohol, and opiates follow a common pattern: short-term coherence relief, rapid reduction of discomfort or uncertainty, and long-term degradation of regulatory capacity.

Nicotine sharpens local attentional coherence through cholinergic agonism but creates dependence: the system's baseline attentional regulation recalibrates around nicotine's effects, so that withdrawal produces attentional incoherence worse than pre-use baseline. The net effect over time is reduced autonomous regulatory capacity.

Caffeine increases alertness and task-directed coherence through adenosine receptor blockade. Its coherence costs are relatively modest compared to other substances, but chronic use produces tolerance (the baseline shifts) and dependence (withdrawal produces cognitive fog and fatigue that would not have existed without chronic use).

Alcohol acutely reduces IES through GABAergic enhancement and glutamatergic suppression — the neurochemical equivalent of lowering the system's sensitivity to its own incoherence. This is why alcohol feels relieving: the system genuinely registers less coherence distress. But the relief is signal suppression, not resolution. Integration is impaired during intoxication; memory consolidation is disrupted; emotional processing is short-circuited. Chronic use progressively damages the regulatory infrastructure itself — the physiological coherence base (Appendix A, §A.1) upon which all higher-level integration depends.

Opiates produce the most extreme form of signal suppression: they reduce not merely threat signaling but the felt weight of all coherence dynamics, producing a state of apparent integration that is actually regulatory shutdown. The system feels coherent because it feels nothing — a pharmacological simulacrum of peace that masks deepening structural fragmentation. The addictive power of opiates reflects the intensity of the coherence relief they provide; the destructive power reflects the comprehensiveness of the signal suppression that produces it.

The widespread use of these substances reflects unmet coherence needs rather than moral failure. In environments where IES is chronically elevated and coherence support is absent (Section 11.4), self-medication with substances that provide immediate IES reduction is a predictable — indeed, from the system's local perspective, rational — response. The problem is not the response but the conditions that make it necessary.

F.7 Ethical and Clinical Implications

From a CU perspective, the evaluative stance toward psychoactive substances is neither prohibitionist nor permissive. It is structural:

Medication is not opposed to therapy; it is a coherence tool operating at a different level. Overuse reflects unresolved coherence conflict that the substance manages rather than resolves. Underuse reflects moralization of distress — the belief that suffering should be endured rather than modulated, which increases IES without any corresponding coherence benefit.

The ethical criterion is not abstinence, pharmacological purity, or subjective happiness. It is whether the intervention supports sustainable coherence without escalating tradeoffs — whether it enables the system's own coherence drive to operate more effectively or whether it substitutes pharmacological regulation for the structural integration that long-term viability requires.

Appendix F — Developmental Attractor Dynamics of Psychological Coherence

This appendix presents a developmental model of psychological coherence framed in terms of attractor dynamics. Rather than treating development as a sequence of moral stages or a fixed hierarchy, this model describes how the deepest regulating attractor in a psychological system tends to shift over time — shaping identity, motivation, moral reasoning, and vulnerability to breakdown.

The central claim is that psychological maturity consists not in acquiring specific beliefs, virtues, or personality traits but in developing internal coherence attractors capable of stabilizing action and meaning independently of external regulation.

G.1 Attractors and Psychological Regulation

In dynamical systems terms, an attractor is a state or region toward which a system tends to evolve, especially under perturbation. In psychology, attractors correspond to the regulatory patterns that dominate under stress — what the system "falls back on" when coherence is threatened.

A system's deepest attractor is not its most frequently accessed state but the one that dominates regulation under uncertainty or threat, organizes identity coherence (which challenges are experienced as identity-threatening depends on what the system is organized around), constrains moral reasoning and self-justification (the system evaluates moral situations from the perspective of its deepest attractor), and shapes meaning-map structure (the meaning map Φ is organized to protect and serve the deepest attractor).

Development can be understood as changes in attractor dominance — shifts in which regulatory pattern is deepest — rather than as linear accumulation of skills, knowledge, or moral sophistication. This is why development is nonlinear: shifts in attractor dominance require passing through the destabilized region between basins (the separatrix-crossing of Section 8.6), and not all systems complete the transition.

G.2 Profile 1 — External Attunement Dominant (Infancy)

In early development, coherence is entirely externally regulated. The infant has no stable internal attractors. Regulatory stability depends on coupling with caregivers who provide physiological, emotional, and attentional regulation (Section 6.1, Section 11.1.1).

This profile is fully normative and necessary. Psychological viability at this stage requires remaining coupled to external regulation. The system's meaning space M is minimal and almost entirely structured by the caregiver's regulation — the infant experiences the world through the coherence field the caregiver maintains.

Coherence architecture: No independent attractor structure. Viability region V is jointly maintained by the caregiver—infant dyad. Separation from the caregiver is not merely distressing but constitutes approach toward the boundary of V.

Failure mode: Inadequate caregiving (neglect, abuse, inconsistency) deprives the system of the regulatory scaffolding it needs to begin constructing internal attractors. The developmental consequences are severe: the system may never develop the physiological foundation for affect tolerance (Section 8.2.3), and its subsequent attractor development may be permanently constrained by the impoverished regulatory architecture this period produced.

G.3 Profile 2 — Social Approval Dominant (Childhood → Early Adolescence)

As development proceeds, social belonging replaces the individual caregiver as the primary regulatory field. Identity, truth, and morality are organized around group norms. The system's deepest attractor becomes social approval — the maintenance of belonging, acceptance, and status within the relevant group.

Coherence architecture: The meaning map Φ is structured to track social signals — approval, rejection, inclusion, exclusion. Beliefs are evaluated not primarily by their accuracy but by their social consequences. Morality is imitative: what is right is what the group endorses. Coherence is maintained through alignment with the shared coherence field (CU-Ψ12).

Characteristic functioning: In this profile, belonging overrides accuracy (the system will believe inaccurate things rather than risk social exclusion), morality is conventional (Kohlberg's Stages 3–4), conflict with the group threatens coherence directly (disagreement is experienced not as intellectual difference but as identity threat), and social approval functions as the deepest attractor (the system organizes its meaning map to maximize approval and minimize rejection).

Prevalence: This profile remains adaptive in many social environments and often persists into adulthood. A substantial proportion of adults — perhaps the majority — operate primarily from this attractor, and many function adequately across the full range of ordinary life demands. The profile becomes problematic primarily when social norms conflict with reality, when the system is embedded in a dysfunctional shared coherence field (Section 10.5), or when life demands individual judgment that social consensus cannot provide.

Failure mode: Excessive dependence on social approval produces vulnerability to group-level dysfunction (conformity, obedience, radicalization), inability to maintain coherence when group membership is lost or group norms conflict, and suppression of individual perception and moral judgment in favor of group alignment.

G.4 Profile 3 — Self-Image / Autonomy Dominant (Late Adolescence → Adulthood)

Internal attractors begin to form. Identity becomes partially independent of group norms. Boundaries strengthen. Autonomy and self-consistency become central regulatory concerns. The system can now maintain coherence through self-referential constraint enforcement (CU-I4) rather than social approval alone.

Coherence architecture: The meaning map Φ develops a self-model with significant independent structure — the system knows what it values, what it wants, and who it is, and can maintain these commitments against social pressure. Truth is selectively pursued: the system values accuracy in domains where it enhances self-image but may resist accuracy where it threatens self-consistency. Coherence is maintained through internal self-model protection.

Characteristic functioning: Autonomy and self-consistency are primary regulatory concerns. Social approval remains important but no longer dominant — the system can tolerate social disapproval when it conflicts with self-image. Moral reasoning incorporates individual judgment but may still be organized around self-interest or self-consistency rather than genuine moral coherence.

Prevalence: Many adults stabilize at this profile and function adequately across the full range of professional, relational, and civic demands. The profile supports effective agency, boundary maintenance, and goal pursuit.

Failure mode: Self-image protection can produce self-deception (CU-Ψ11) when honest self-assessment threatens the self-model. The system may resist growth that requires identity revision, because revision threatens the attractor that provides regulatory stability. This produces the characteristic pattern of the competent but rigid adult — effective within a familiar domain but brittle under novel demands that require identity expansion.

G.5 Profile 4 — Epistemic Coherence Dominant (Minority Emergence)

In some individuals, coherence itself becomes the deepest attractor. Truth, understanding, and internal consistency regulate behavior more strongly than social approval or self-image. The system organizes its meaning map around the demand that Φ be accurate — that the map reflect the territory as faithfully as possible, even when accuracy threatens identity, social position, or emotional comfort.

Coherence architecture: The meaning map Φ is organized primarily around representational accuracy and explanatory coherence. The system's deepest commitment is to the integrity of its own understanding. Self-deception (CU-Ψ11) is experienced not merely as uncomfortable but as a fundamental threat to the system's identity — because the system's identity is organized around epistemic coherence, distortion of Φ is an identity violation.

Characteristic functioning: Social belonging loses regulatory primacy — the system can tolerate social isolation when belonging requires epistemic compromise. Meaning becomes cognitively mediated — the system finds meaning in understanding, explanation, and intellectual coherence rather than in social connection or self-enhancement. Moral reasoning becomes principled rather than conventional — the system evaluates moral claims by their coherence rather than their social endorsement.

Prevalence: This profile is disproportionately observed in neurodivergent individuals (whose reduced reliance on social regulation may facilitate earlier transition to epistemic attractors), scientists, philosophers, and system-builders (whose professional environments reward epistemic coherence), and individuals whose developmental environments made epistemic coherence safer than relational dependence (the system learned to regulate through understanding rather than through belonging because belonging was unreliable or dangerous).

Failure mode: Epistemic dominance without relational integration can produce social vulnerability (the system cannot navigate social demands that require non-epistemic coherence strategies), emotional impoverishment (meaning is found in understanding but not in connection), and a characteristic form of arrogance (the system evaluates others by epistemic standards that most people cannot meet, producing isolation and contempt). The system achieves profound coherence along the epistemic dimension while remaining fragmented along the relational and emotional dimensions.

G.6 Profile 5 — Integrated Coherence: Truth + Compassion (Rare, Integrated Maturity)

At the highest level of integration observed, multiple internal attractors are harmonized. Epistemic coherence and relational attunement are no longer in tension — the system can pursue truth without sacrificing connection, and can maintain connection without sacrificing truth.

Coherence architecture: The meaning map Φ is organized around the integration of multiple coherence dimensions simultaneously. The system does not sacrifice epistemic accuracy for relational comfort, or relational engagement for epistemic purity. It has developed the regulatory capacity to hold the tension between competing coherence demands without resolving the tension through suppression of either dimension.

Characteristic functioning: Truth and compassion integrate structurally — the system can deliver difficult truths with care and can maintain care without flinching from difficult truths. Autonomy and connection reinforce rather than compete — the system's independence is not threatened by intimacy, and its intimacy is not threatened by independence. The individual stabilizes others rather than extracting regulation from them — the system's coherence field is large enough to extend regulatory support to others without depleting its own resources. Agency operates across longer horizons and wider domains — the system can maintain coherent action in the face of ambiguity, competing demands, and uncertain outcomes.

Prevalence: Rare. This profile corresponds to what many traditions describe as wisdom, maturity, or spiritual development — without requiring the metaphysical assumptions those traditions typically carry. It is the developmental direction that CU's psychology describes but does not prescribe: the framework specifies the structural conditions for integrated maturity without claiming that all individuals should or can achieve it.

Connection to CU — Ethics: This profile describes the psychological architecture from which genuine moral agency operates. Systems at Profiles 2–3 can follow moral rules and maintain moral consistency. Systems at Profile 4 can reason about moral principles with integrity. Only systems at Profile 5 can integrate moral reasoning with relational sensitivity, epistemic accuracy with compassionate engagement, principled action with contextual flexibility — the full range of capacities that moral life at its most demanding requires.

G.7 Transitions, Regression, and Context

Attractor dominance is context-sensitive. Stress, trauma, or overwhelming demand can cause regression to earlier profiles — the system falls back to the deepest attractor that is stable under current conditions. A Profile 4 individual under severe social pressure may temporarily reorganize around social approval (Profile 2). A Profile 5 individual under extreme threat may temporarily organize around self-preservation (Profile 3). Development is therefore nonlinear and reversible.

Transitions between profiles require sufficient coherence capacity (the system must be able to tolerate the IES of the transition), environments that do not punish individuation (if the social context penalizes deviation from Profile 2, transition to Profiles 3–5 is actively opposed), tolerable levels of IES (the system cannot reorganize if it is already at the boundary of V), and opportunities for meaning-map revision (the system needs encounters, experiences, or relationships that challenge the current attractor and make the alternative accessible).

Failure to transition is not a moral flaw. It reflects structural constraints — the system's architecture, history, environment, and available support. CU describes development without prescribing it, recognizing that each profile represents a viable coherence strategy under specific conditions and that the conditions for transition are not always present.

G.8 Neurodiversity, Trauma, and Attractor Dynamics

Neurodivergent architectures often alter attractor salience. Systems with reduced reliance on social regulation (autism spectrum) may move toward epistemic coherence dominance (Profile 4) earlier than neurotypical development would predict — not because they have "skipped" social development but because their coherence architecture weights the epistemic dimension more heavily from the outset. Systems with heightened social sensitivity may remain more deeply organized around social approval (Profile 2) but with greater capacity for attunement within that profile.

Trauma can forcibly shift systems toward externally dominant attractors, prioritizing safety and predictability over integration. A system that was developing toward Profile 3 or 4 may, following trauma, reorganize around the most basic regulatory patterns — external attunement (Profile 1) or social approval (Profile 2) — because these provide the regulatory stability the system needs to survive. Healing involves restoring the conditions for internal attractor development rather than "advancing" through stages — the system must first stabilize before it can resume the developmental trajectory that trauma interrupted.

G.9 Implications for Ethics and Meaning

Moral reasoning capacity depends on attractor structure. Systems regulated primarily by social approval (Profile 2) justify actions by reference to group norms: "This is what good people do." Systems regulated by self-image (Profile 3) justify actions by reference to self-consistency: "This is who I am." Systems regulated by epistemic coherence (Profile 4) justify actions by reference to principles: "This is what coherence requires." Systems at integrated maturity (Profile 5) justify actions by reference to the full coherence landscape: "This is what truth, compassion, and the situation jointly demand."

This framework explains persistent moral disagreement without invoking bad faith or ignorance. People at different attractor profiles literally inhabit different moral landscapes — they evaluate moral situations from different structural positions in meaning space, and what counts as a good reason differs systematically across profiles. Understanding this does not excuse moral failure, but it clarifies what moral development requires: not merely better information or stronger principles, but structural reorganization of the system's deepest regulatory dynamics.

Self-deception (CU-Ψ11) functions as an attractor-protective strategy: when truths threaten the deepest attractor, meaning maps distort to preserve coherence at the cost of accuracy. The specific form of self-deception varies by profile: Profile 2 systems deceive themselves about group-incongruent perceptions; Profile 3 systems deceive themselves about self-image-threatening facts; Profile 4 systems deceive themselves about relationally or emotionally inconvenient truths. Only at Profile 5 is the system's architecture oriented toward minimizing self-deception itself — making the avoidance of Φ-distortion a core regulatory commitment rather than a secondary consideration.

These dynamics provide the psychological foundation for the ethical framework developed in CU — Ethics, where moral permissibility is constrained by coherence preservation and avoidance of self-deception.

Appendix G — Meaning, Culture, and the Modern Coherence Crisis

This appendix situates individual psychology within contemporary cultural conditions, extending the analysis of Section 11.4 with additional specificity about the mechanisms through which modern environments produce population-level coherence degradation.

H.1 The Structural Diagnosis

The modern mental health crisis is not primarily a crisis of individual psychology. It is a coherence crisis in which the shared structures that historically supported individual regulation — cultural narratives, institutional trust, community belonging, stable social roles, intergenerational meaning transmission — have degraded faster than individual or collective systems can compensate.

Section 11.4 identified four mechanisms of modern IES generation (informational density, social comparison at scale, meaning structure erosion, algorithmic engagement optimization) and the systematic degradation of Rungs 22–26 (shared representations, coordination dynamics, norms, institutions, culture). This appendix develops the implications.

H.2 Meaning as Long-Horizon Coherence Under Threat

Meaning (Rung 21) is the longest-horizon coherence signal — the system's assessment of whether its trajectory has direction, purpose, and evaluative weight that extends beyond immediate needs (Section 9.4). Meaning requires temporal depth: the capacity to connect past experience, present action, and future orientation into an integrated narrative.

Modern conditions systematically attack temporal depth. Digital environments fragment attention into micro-intervals. Economic precarity makes long-range planning feel futile. Cultural fragmentation eliminates shared frameworks within which individual meaning could be situated. The result is a population increasingly confined to short-horizon coherence — managing moment-to-moment demands without the stabilizing structure of longer-horizon meaning.

The phenomenological consequences are well-documented: the epidemic of "emptiness" and "flatness" reported in clinical settings, the rise of "deaths of despair" (Case & Deaton, 2015, 2020), the widespread sense that life lacks direction or purpose even among materially comfortable populations. These are not symptoms of individual pathology. They are the subjective registration of meaning-structure degradation — the system's coherence drive (CU-Ψ5) detecting that long-horizon integration is unavailable.

H.3 The Overload of Coherence Drive

Coherence drive (CU-Ψ5) is constitutive and continuous — it cannot be switched off. In environments where coherence challenges are manageable and coherence support is available, the drive produces adaptive behavior: exploration, learning, integration, meaning-making. In environments where coherence challenges overwhelm capacity and coherence support is absent, the same drive produces maladaptive compensation: compulsive information-seeking that increases rather than reduces uncertainty, social media engagement that amplifies rather than resolves comparison anxiety, ideological commitment that simplifies rather than integrates complexity, and substance use that suppresses rather than addresses distress.

These responses are structurally identical to the compensatory strategies described throughout the paper (Sections 4.5, 4.5, 6.4, 9.5). The difference is that modern environments produce them at population scale — not because modern humans are psychologically weaker than their predecessors but because the coherence demands of modern environments are structurally unprecedented and the coherence support infrastructure that historically modulated those demands has deteriorated.

H.4 The Limits of Individual Therapy Under Collective Incoherence

Individual therapy remains necessary and valuable. But the CU framework makes visible a fundamental limitation: therapy operates on individual systems within a collective context, and when the collective context is itself incoherent, individual repair faces structural headwinds.

A therapist can help a patient restructure her meaning map, develop more effective regulatory strategies, and restore integrative capacity. But if the patient returns from each session to an environment that fragments attention, erodes trust, undermines meaning, and amplifies comparison anxiety, the restored coherence faces continuous degradation from the same environmental forces that produced the original breakdown.

This is not an argument against therapy. It is an argument that therapy alone — individual intervention without collective reorganization — cannot resolve a crisis whose roots are collective. The CU framework specifies what collective reorganization requires: institutional reform that restores the legitimacy and function of shared regulatory structures (Rung 25), community reconstruction that rebuilds the distributed coherence infrastructure on which individual regulation depends (Rungs 22–24), technology design that respects coherence constraints rather than exploiting coherence drive for engagement and profit (CU-Ψ5, Section 11.4.1), and cultural innovation that creates new shared meaning structures adequate to present conditions (Rung 26, CU-CL-8).

H.5 Toward Coherence-Informed Design

The CU framework generates specific design principles for environments, institutions, and technologies:

Environments should support the coherence hierarchy — providing physiological regulation (exercise, nature, sleep), emotional safety (community, belonging), cognitive integration (education, reflection), identity coherence (stable roles, meaningful work), and meaning construction (narrative, purpose, contribution). Environments that systematically undermine any level of this hierarchy — as many modern workplaces, schools, and digital environments do — produce population-level IES regardless of individual resilience.

Institutions should serve as coherence scaffolding — reducing individual regulatory burden by providing predictable, trustworthy, and legitimate frameworks for coordination. When institutions serve their own perpetuation rather than their coherence function, they become extraction systems (Section 10.3) that maintain structural form while hollowing out structural function.

Technologies should be evaluated by their coherence impact — not merely by their efficiency, engagement metrics, or profit potential.

Technologies that capture coherence drive (CU-Ψ5) and redirect it toward short-horizon satisfaction while degrading long-horizon integration are coherence-destructive regardless of how popular they are or how much revenue they generate. The CU framework provides a principled basis for this evaluation: does the technology support the user's capacity for integrated regulation across domains and timescales, or does it exploit the user's coherence drive for purposes that do not serve the user's coherence?

H.6 Conclusion

The modern coherence crisis is real, structural, and consequential. It manifests as individual suffering — anxiety, depression, addiction, meaninglessness — but its roots are collective: the degradation of shared coherence fields under conditions that exceed their adaptive capacity.

Understanding this crisis through the CU framework transforms the response from symptom management to structural intervention. The task is not merely to treat the individuals who are suffering but to rebuild the coherence infrastructure — cultural, institutional, technological — within which individual coherence can be sustained. This is the largest practical implication of the psychological framework this paper has developed, and it connects directly to the institutional, ethical, and technological analyses pursued in CU — Ethics and CU — AI.

Appendix H: Referenced Principles from the CU Framework

This appendix compiles all CU principles referenced in this paper, with their definitions from CU — Foundations and the principle definitions introduced in this paper. Definitions are reproduced for standalone intelligibility; readers are referred to the source documents for full derivation and discussion.

I.1 Foundational Principles (CU-FP)

Source: CU — Foundations, Part I.

CU-FP1 — Coherence as a Transcendental Condition. Wherever persistence, structure, meaning, agency, or normativity appear, coherence is a necessary condition of their possibility. *[In this paper: Grounds the claim that psychological coherence is not optional but structurally required for any form of minded existence]*

CU-FP2 — Coherence Admits of Degree and Direction. Coherence is graded, not binary, and systems move through coherence landscapes along coherence gradients. *[In this paper: Enables the dimensional approach to mental health — coherence is not present or absent but higher or lower across multiple domains]*

CU-FP3 — Constraint Is Essential to Coherence. Coherence without constraint collapses into fantasy; constraint without coherence collapses into noise. *[In this paper: Explains why protective factors and stressors are structurally necessary for psychological development, not merely environmental inputs]*

CU-FP4 — Multi-Scale Coherence (LGCP). Coherence is defined across nested scales: local, relational, global, and temporal. *[In this paper: Grounds the multi-domain coherence model — emotional, narrative, relational, motivational, and meaning coherence must be jointly satisfiable]*

CU-FP5 — Coherence Is Non-Reductive. Coherence at one level cannot be reduced to coherence at another. *[In this paper: Establishes that psychological coherence is irreducible to neurological function — the anti--reductionist claim]*

CU-FP7 — Coherence Collapse. When coherence drops below a viability threshold, the system fragments into components that retain coherence at lower scales. *[In this paper: Models dissociation, psychotic fragmentation, and identity collapse as structural phenomena]*

CU-FP8 — Identity as Constraint-Preserved Coherence. Identity is the persistence of self-enforcing viability constraints across irreversible internal transformation. *[In this paper: Grounds the model of identity coherence across developmental change and trauma]*

I.2 Dynamics Principles (CU-D)

Source: CU — Foundations, Part II.

CU-D1 — The Universal Flow Equation. All coherent systems evolve according to a canonical update rule driven by coherence gradients and modulated by constraint. *[In this paper: The formal basis for modeling psychological development, therapy, and crisis]*

CU-D2 — Coherence Drive. A system with coherence above viability minimum maintains an intrinsic gradient toward higher coherence. *[In this paper: Reframed as psychological motivation — the inherent directedness toward integration that underlies all motivated behavior]*

CU-D3 — Biological Coherence Drive. Biological systems maintain coherence through active self-repair and constraint satisfaction. *[In this paper: The biological substrate from which psychological coherence drive (CU-Ψ5) emerges]*

CU-D4 — Coherence Gradients. At each point in state space, the coherence gradient defines the direction of maximal coherence increase. *[In this paper: Models the intuitive sense of "what would help" — the felt directionality of psychological repair]*

CU-D6 — Multi-Timescale Coherence. Coherence operates across multiple timescales simultaneously. *[In this paper: Explains why short-term coping strategies can undermine long-term integration, and why developmental trajectories span decades]*

CU-D7 — Novelty via Constraint Navigation. Genuine novelty arises not from the absence of constraint but from navigation within constraint landscapes. *[In this paper: Models creativity, therapeutic breakthrough, and identity transformation]*

CU-D8 — Repair over Optimization. Coherent systems are oriented toward repair of damaged coherence rather than optimization of arbitrary objectives. *[In this paper: The structural basis for the claim that therapy is repair, not optimization]*

CU-D9 — Multi-Scale Failure Modes. Coherence can fail at any scale, and failure at one scale propagates to others. *[In this paper: Models cascading psychological breakdown — how loss at one domain destabilizes others]*

CU-D10 — Memory as Path-Dependent Coherence. A system's current coherence state reflects its entire history of coherence maintenance and failure. *[In this paper: Grounds the role of autobiographical memory in identity coherence and explains why trauma has lasting structural effects]*

I.3 Consciousness Conditions (CU-C)

Source: CU — Foundations, Part IV.

CU-C1 — Global Integrative Coherence. Consciousness requires that information be globally integrated across the system. *[In this paper: The structural requirement for unified experience that dissociation violates]*

CU-C3 — Valence as Ineliminable Self-Constraint. Conscious systems necessarily experience their own states as positive or negative. *[In this paper: Grounds the claim that affect is not epiphenomenal but structurally constitutive of conscious experience]*

CU-C6 — World-Constrained Coherence. Consciousness is not free-floating but constrained by interaction with an external world. *[In this paper: Explains why reality-testing is constitutive of healthy psychological function]*

CU-C7 — Intrinsic Normative Standing. Systems satisfying all consciousness conditions possess normative standing — their coherence matters, not merely instrumentally. *[In this paper: Grounds the ethical dimension of mental health]*

I.4 Psychological Principles (CU-Ψ)

Source: Introduced in this paper.

CU-Ψ1 — Meaning Space. Psychological coherence operates within a structured space of meaning, where dimensions correspond to domains of psychological integration (emotional, narrative, relational, motivational, value, identity, existential).

CU-Ψ2 — Meaning Maps. An individual's current psychological state is a position in meaning space, and their developmental trajectory is a path through it. Meaning maps are the representational structures that track this position.

CU-Ψ3 — Field Coherence Score. A composite measure of psychological coherence across all meaning-space dimensions, providing a single index of overall psychological integration.

CU-Ψ4 — Inverse Entropic Stress. Psychological entropy — the disorganization of meaning structures — generates subjective distress proportional to the degree of incoherence. Anxiety, depression, and meaninglessness are structural signals, not merely chemical states.

CU-Ψ5 — Coherence Drive. The psychological expression of CU-D2: the inherent directedness of psychological systems toward greater integration, experienced as the pursuit of meaning, connection, and purpose.

CU-Ψ6 — Local–Global Tension. Psychological coherence at one scale may conflict with coherence at another (e.g., short-term emotional regulation vs. long-term identity integration), generating characteristic psychological tensions.

CU-Ψ7 — Coherence Repair. The capacity for self-directed repair of psychological coherence following perturbation — the basis of resilience, coping, and therapeutic change.

CU-Ψ8 — Coherence Fragmentation. When psychological coherence drops below viability minimum, the system fragments into semi-autonomous subsystems — the structural model of dissociation and identity disorganization.

CU-Ψ9 — Developmental Attractors. Psychological development follows attractor dynamics: stable configurations of coherence that resist small perturbations but can undergo phase transitions under sufficient stress or growth.

CU-Ψ10 — Attachment as Coherence Regulation. Attachment relationships serve as external coherence regulators: the capacity for self-regulation develops through internalization of co-regulatory patterns.

CU-Ψ11 — Self-Deception. The psychological mechanism by which an agent maintains the appearance of coherence while actual coherence degrades — the central pathology of psychological incoherence.

CU-Ψ12 — Coherence Infrastructure. The cultural, institutional, and technological systems that support or undermine individual psychological coherence. The modern coherence crisis reflects degradation of this infrastructure.

I.5 Other Referenced Principles

CU-V1 — Self-Maintenance Under Constraint. A system satisfies V1 if it actively maintains its own coherence against perturbation. *[In this paper: The viability condition that defines the boundary between adaptive and pathological coping]*

CU-V7 — Non-Derivative Normative Standing. Systems satisfying all viability conditions possess inherent normative standing. *[In this paper: Grounds the claim that mental health is not merely instrumental but a matter of intrinsic value]*

CU-E-5 — Self-Deception as Structural Moral Failure. Self-deception corrupts the agent's capacity for honest self-assessment. *[In this paper: The ethical dimension of CU-Ψ11 — self-deception is both psychologically and morally pathological]*

CU-L6 — Non-Monotonic Consequence. Adding information can defeat previously warranted conclusions. *[In this paper: Models the revisability of psychological self-understanding — new experience can restructure meaning]*

CU-Ep4 — Epistemic Coherence. Justified belief requires coherence across evidence, inference, and background commitment. *[In this paper: The epistemic dimension of psychological health — healthy cognition tracks reality]*

About the Author

Gaura Kiśora Dās Rader was raised from birth in a Gaudiya Vaishnava spiritual community, where daily temple practice shaped his earliest development. At five, he entered a traditional gurukula — a residential school rooted in pre-dawn prayer, chanting, and the study of ancient scriptures — and remained in contemplative education through his mid-teens. Shortly after he turned 18, he dedicated himself to full-time monastic life as a teacher and practitioner, a path he followed into his late twenties.

He then pursued formal academic training — an MA in Philosophy from the University of Florida and doctoral work in Social Psychology at Ohio University — not as a departure from his contemplative formation but as an effort to build the conceptual and empirical tools it lacked. His research spans the philosophy of logic, moral philosophy, and moral psychology.

Due to circumstances in his personal life, Gaura was forced to leave the doctoral path. But the distance from academia turned out to be a blessing in disguise. Stepping away, he could finally see what he couldn't from inside the institution — the harm that the methodology and assumptions of scientific materialism were doing to the project of human inquiry and the project of human progress. Coherence Universalism grew out of that clarity: not as an academic exercise, but as an integrative response to limitations he had lived from both contemplative and scholarly sides.

Gaura is the founder and Director of Research at the Heaven≡Earth Foundation, a research and public-benefit organization based in Athens, Ohio dedicated to advancing coherence through the integration of scientific insight, spiritual understanding, and practical systems. He teaches Embodied Coherence — a movement practice integrating rope flow, qigong, yoga, and dance — in Athens, where he lives with his family. The Coherence Universalism series represents the culmination of a lifelong journey.

For the complete Coherence Universalism series and supporting materials, visit heavenearthfoundation.org.

www.ingramcontent.com/pod-product-compliance
Lightning Source LLC
LaVergne TN
LVHW091135080826
845145LV00008B/2161

* 9 7 8 1 9 7 2 4 2 9 0 4 4 *